OKLAHOMA TRIVIA

OKLAHOMA TRIVIA

COMPILED BY ERNIE COUCH

Rutledge Hill Press®
Nashville, Tennessee

Published in Nashville, Tennessee, by Rutledge Hill Press, Inc.,
211 Seventh Avenue North, Nashville, Tennessee 37219.
Distributed in Canada by H. B. Fenn & Company, Ltd., 34 Nixon Road,
Bolton, Ontario, L7E 1W2.

Library of Congress Cataloging-in-Publication Data
Couch, Ernie, 1949–
    Oklahoma trivia / complied by Ernie Couch.
        p.   cm.
    ISBN 1-55853-732-5
    1. Oklahoma—Miscellanea.   2. Oklahoma—History—Miscellanea.
I. Title.
F694.6.C68   1999   99-13904
976.6—dc21   CIP

Printed in the United States of America
1 2 3 4 5 6 7 8 9—02 01 00 99

PREFACE

Few states can boast of so colorful a heritage or so diversified a land and people as Oklahoma. It would be impossible to capture in print all the elements that have blended together to form this unique state. Throughout its fascinating history, Oklahoma has stood at the forefront of leadership, ingenuity, and development. Some of the highlights of this rich heritage, both the known and the not-so-well-known, are collected within these pages.

Oklahoma Trivia is designed to be informative, educational, and entertaining. But most of all, I hope you will be motivated to learn more about the great state of Oklahoma.

—Ernie Couch

To
Jack & Ann Brown, Grace Powell,
and
the great people of Oklahoma

TABLE OF CONTENTS

GEOGRAPHY

C H A P T E R   O N E

Q. What is the meaning of the Choctaw expression *oklahoma*?

A. "Red people."

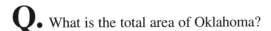

Q. Where was the Creek (Muscogee Nation) Council House constructed in 1878?

A. Okmulgee.

Q. What is the total area of Oklahoma?

A. 69,919 square miles.

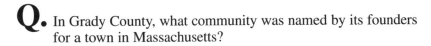

Q. In Grady County, what community was named by its founders for a town in Massachusetts?

A. Pocasset.

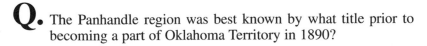

Q. The Panhandle region was best known by what title prior to becoming a part of Oklahoma Territory in 1890?

A. No-Man's-Land.

Q. In what county can you visit the town of Gene Autry?

A. Carter.

Q. Northeastern State University maintains campuses in what three towns?

A. Tahlequah, Tulsa, and Muskogee.

Q. By what previous name was Grant known?

A. Tailholt.

Q. What river serves as the southern boundary of Oklahoma?

A. Red River.

Q. Where was Oklahoma's first rural mail route established in 1900 to service a 31-square-mile area with 70 residents?

A. Hennessey.

Q. What small town, with a population of less than 25 people, is the only community in the state on mountain standard time?

A. Keaton.

Q. In Pontotoc County, what town is named for the daughter of the area's pioneer mail carrier and settler?

A. Ada (daughter of Jeff Reed).

Q. What two Oklahoma ports on the Arkansas River McClellan-Kerr Waterway are designated as foreign trade zones?

A. Muskogee and Catoosa.

Q. Where is the Chisholm Trail Museum?

A. Kingfisher.

Q. By what Creek Indian name was Haskell first known?

A. SawOkla.

Q. Shortly after statehood, what title was given to the proposal to establish a new capital at the geographical center of the state?

A. The "New Jerusalem" plan.

Q. Near what community may one see the only remaining pioneer sod house in the state?

A. Cleo Springs.

Q. For a few months during the coming of the railroads, Blackwell consolidated under the name of what rival town?

A. Parker.

Q. Where is the Five Civilized Tribes Museum and Center for the Study of Indian Territory?

A. Muskogee.

Q. What was the official name of the area known as the Cherokee Strip?

A. Cherokee Outlet.

Q. What town served as the capital of the Territory of Oklahoma?

A. Guthrie.

Q. Where did oil baron Ernest Whitworth Marland complete construction on his 55-room, 30,388-square-foot "Place on the Prairie" in 1928?

A. Ponca City.

Q. Mentow, Les Mentous, Campbell, and Illinois are all former names of what Sequoyah County town?

A. Gore.

Q. In 1917, what Panhandle town packed up and collectively moved six miles south to a new site that would evolve into Follet, Texas?

A. South Ivanhoe.

Q. Who founded the town of Pauls Valley in 1857?

A. Smith Paul.

Q. In Carter County, what now-vanished town east of Spiro was the capital of the northern district of the Choctaw Nation?

A. Skullyville.

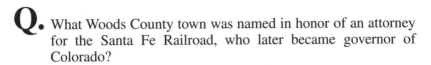

Q. What Woods County town was named in honor of an attorney for the Santa Fe Railroad, who later became governor of Colorado?

A. Alva (for Alva B. Adams).

Q. Where is the Homesteaders Monument, which bears the names of pioneers who participated in the 1893 Cherokee Strip Land Run?

A. Medford.

Q. Situated at the very southeastern corner of the state, what is the elevation of the lowest point in Oklahoma?

A. 324 feet above sea level.

Q. What LeFlore County town was at one time known as Choctaw City?

A. Heavener.

Q. "Ten miles from town" is the meaning of what Choctaw place-name?

A. Pocola (ten miles from Fort Smith, Arkansas).

Q. The community of Bugtussle is in what county?

A. Pittsburg.

Q. At an 1887 meeting in Beaver City, residents of the Panhandle area attempted to create a government for what proposed territory?

A. Cimarron.

Q. Originally located two miles to the north, Coyle was first known by what name?

A. Iowa City.

Q. Where does Oklahoma rank in size among the other states?

A. 18th.

Q. What town in southern Tulsa County was named for the chairman of the 1893 Dawes Commission?

A. Bixby (for Tams Bixby).

Q. Where is the National Cowboy Hall of Fame?

A. Oklahoma City.

Q. From the 1830s to 1863, where was the capital of the Choctaw Nation?

A. Doaksville.

Q. What Wagoner County town was named by the Creek for an ancestral town in Georgia?

A. Coweta.

Q. In whose honor is Weatherford's airport named?

A. General Thomas P. Stafford.

Q. What do the counties of Atoka, Muskogee, Nowata, Okmulgee, Wagoner, Pawnee, Kingfisher, Tulsa, Woodward, and Beaver share in common with their respective county seats?

A. The same name.

Q. In what town is Southeastern Oklahoma State University?

A. Durant.

Q. From where were the solid mahogany furnishings of the State Supreme Court courtroom imported in 1918?

A. The West Indies.

Q. The 1933 Creek settlement of Adams Springs was the precursor of what present-day town?

A. Sand Springs.

Q. What Lincoln County town, founded in 1891, was named in honor of a Kansan who served as assistant secretary of the interior from 1889 to 1893?

A. Chandler (for George Chandler).

Q. In what county is the town of Corn?

A. Washita.

Q. What is the meaning of the Cherokee place-name Oologah in Rogers County?

A. "Dark cloud."

Q. The University of Science and Arts of Oklahoma, which is the only publicly funded liberal arts university in the state, is in what town?

A. Chickasha.

Q. What town is officially known as "the Czech Capital of Oklahoma"?

A. Yukon.

Q. Early explorers gave what name to the north-south strip of rough, timbered country that ran through the central part of the state?

A. The Cross Timbers.

Q. What is the most southeastern town in the state?

A. Tom.

Q. Following a decision of the United States Supreme Court, what county was attached to Oklahoma Territory?

A. Greer.

Q. By what name was Ponca City first known?

A. New Ponca.

Q. What Oklahoma City suburb's original town charter forbade theaters, pool halls, beauty salons, and the sale of tobacco or intoxicants?

A. Bethany.

Q. Where is the Choctaw Nation Council House?

A. Tuskahoma.

Q. "Those who camp at a distance," or "wild," is the meaning of what Oklahoma place-name?

A. Seminole.

Q. What Beckham County town is home to a unique museum that deals with the history of the 100th meridian?

A. Erick.

Q. For whom was Cleveland in Pawnee County named?

A. President Grover Cleveland.

———⚬⚬⚬———

Q. What is the greatest east-west distance across Oklahoma?

A. 464 miles (747 kilometers).

———⚬⚬⚬———

Q. Where is the largest Scottish rite temple in the world?

A. Guthrie.

———⚬⚬⚬———

Q. What Carter County town was named for a United States marshal who served the area during territorial days?

A. Weatherford (for William J. Weatherford).

———⚬⚬⚬———

Q. In what county may one visit the community of Cookietown?

A. Cotton.

———⚬⚬⚬———

Q. What Carter County town, founded in 1903, was named for a federal judge?

A. Clinton (for Judge Clinton F. Irwin).

———⚬⚬⚬———

Q. Anadarko is the seat of what county?

A. Caddo.

Q. When a flood forced founding settlers to move their possessions up the slope of a nearby hill, what Jackson County town was given a place-name with the supposed meaning of "higher ground"?

A. Altus.

———∞———

Q. A trading post called Jimtown evolved into what northeastern Oklahoma town?

A. Miami.

———∞———

Q. The Panhandle of Oklahoma is made up of what three counties?

A. Cimarron, Texas, and Beaver.

———∞———

Q. Prior to a mapmaker's spelling error, Checotah was known by what name?

A. Checote (Checote Switch).

———∞———

Q. What southwestern Ottawa County town is said to have been named for a river made famous in a Robert Burns poem?

A. Afton.

———∞———

Q. Where is the Choctaw Indian Hospital?

A. Talihina.

Q. What small 1870 settlement was the forerunner of present-day Vinita?

A. Downingville.

———— ✸ ————

Q. Clem Rogers, for whom Rogers County was named, was what relationship to Will Rogers?

A. Father.

———— ✸ ————

Q. What was the name of the southern section of territory land opened to settlers in December 1906?

A. Big Pasture.

———— ✸ ————

Q. The United States Naval Ammunition Depot is in what county?

A. Pittsburg.

———— ✸ ————

Q. A ford established on the Cimarron River by Tom Mann gave rise to the name of what Creek County town?

A. Mannsford.

———— ✸ ————

Q. What is the greatest north-south distance across Oklahoma?

A. 230 miles (370 kilometers).

———— ✸ ————

Q. Where is Carl Albert State College?

A. Poteau.

Q. What Kingfisher County town is named for a pioneer freight hauler who was killed by Indians along the Chisholm Trail?

A. Hennessey (for Pat Hennessey).

———

Q. Oklahoma is divided into how many counties?

A. 77.

———

Q. In 1898, what eastern Lincoln County town moved about a mile south and a mile east to take advantage of the coming railroad?

A. Stroud.

———

Q. What Beckham County town was originally named Busch in honor of the St. Louis brewmaster, Adolphus Busch?

A. Elk City.

———

Q. Present-day highway US 81 basically follows or parallels what famous 1800s cattle trail as it crosses Oklahoma?

A. Chisholm Trail.

———

Q. Portions of Oklahoma City are found in what five counties?

A. Canadian, Cleveland, McClain, Oklahoma, and Pottawatomie.

———

Q. What Beaver County town was named for a Chicago banker?

A. Forgan (for James B. Forgan).

Q. Where is Oral Roberts University?

A. Tulsa.

Q. In Carter County, what town is named for a circus executive?

A. Ringling (for John Ringling).

Q. Waurika was first known by what name?

A. Monika.

Q. What town started as a tent city in 1902 at the juncture of the Frisco Railroad and the Arkansas & Choctaw's Grant logging spur?

A. Hugo.

Q. In the Choctaw language, what is the meaning of the name of the LeFlore County town Talihina, which grew up along the Frisco Railroad?

A. "Iron road."

Q. Wilburton is the seat of what county?

A. Latimer.

Q. The Native-American word *winneoka*, meaning "good water," or "sweet water," has been corrupted into what present-day Oklahoma place-name?

A. Waynoka.

Q. What cemetery northeast of Spiro marks the location of one of the first settlements of relocated Native Americans in Indian Territory?

A. Skullyville Cemetery.

Q. Frogville is in what county?

A. Choctaw.

Q. What is the meaning of the Delaware word *no-we-ata* from which the place-name Nowata is derived?

A. "Welcome."

Q. Clayton is the seat of what county?

A. Pushmataha.

Q. What is the meaning of the Cherokee place-name Catoosa?

A. "On the hill."

Q. In Pittsburg County, what community is known as "Little Italy"?

A. Krebs.

Q. For what 1870s surveyor was Norman named?

A. Abner Ernest Norman.

Q. Where is the Railroad Museum of Oklahoma?

A. Enid.

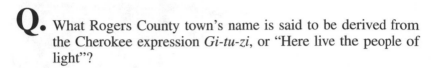

Q. What Rogers County town's name is said to be derived from the Cherokee expression *Gi-tu-zi*, or "Here live the people of light"?

A. Catoosa.

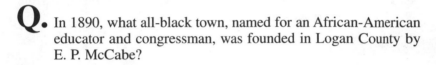

Q. In 1890, what all-black town, named for an African-American educator and congressman, was founded in Logan County by E. P. McCabe?

A. Langston (for John M. Langston).

Q. Where is Northwestern Oklahoma State University?

A. Alva.

Q. Located just north of Geary, the grave of Jesse Chisholm is at what old campsite along the trail that bore his name?

A. Left Hand Spring Camp.

Q. Peery and Moneka are former names of what Jefferson County town?

A. Waurika.

Q. In the Seminole language, what is the meaning of the place-name Wewoka?

A. "Barking waters."

———————

Q. What famous pioneer trail transversed Cimarron Country?

A. Old Santa Fe Trail.

———————

Q. In what eastern county do you find Westville?

A. Adair County.

———————

Q. King's post office, established in 1889 and relocated two miles to the east the following year, was given what new name in honor of a federal territorial judge?

A. Dale (for Judge Frank Dale of Guthrie).

———————

Q. In the United States, Oklahoma City ranks third for largest land area behind what two cities?

A. Juneau, Alaska, and Jacksonville, Florida.

———————

Q. Idabel, named for a local Choctaw citizen's daughters, Ida and Belle, was formerly known by what name?

A. Mitchell.

———————

Q. Madill is the seat of what county?

A. Marshall.

Q. What was the name of the camping site where the town of Tishomingo was founded?

A. Good Springs.

Q. Located just a little northwest of present-day Tuskahoma, what was the name of the original Choctaw Nation's capital?

A. Nunih Wayah.

Q. Tar River was the forerunner of what Ottawa County community?

A. Cardin.

Q. What Mayes County town bears the name of a scout with Lewis and Clark who later became a licensed trader with the Osage?

A. Pryor (for Nathaniel Pryor).

Q. What town is home to Connors State College?

A. Warner.

Q. In 1892, Cushing was founded on the lands of what ranch?

A. Turkey Track Ranch.

Q. What town, southeast of Tulsa, is said to have been named for a colorful and popular train dispatcher who lived in Parsons, Kansas?

A. Wagoner (for "Bigfoot" Wagoner).

Q. Where is the large Tinker Air Force base?

A. Oklahoma City (near Midwest City).

Q. Coretta Switch, North Muskogee, and Rex are all former names of what Wagoner County town?

A. Okay.

Q. North Fork Town, later renamed Migco for the Creek word meaning "chief," evolved into what McIntosh County town?

A. Eufaula.

Q. In 1855, what now-vanished town on the Texas Road became the seat of Tobusksy County in the Choctaw Nation?

A. Perryville.

Q. Buffalo is the seat of what county?

A. Harper.

Q. Baptist missionary Reverend J. S. Murrow founded what town in 1867?

A. Atoka.

Q. What important Choctaw-Chickasaw pioneer town, in present-day Atoka County, saw its heyday in the mid-1800s, only to disappear after being bypassed by the railroad in 1872?

A. Boggy Depot.

Q. The Indian name of the principal chief of the Cherokees from 1875 to 1879 is the source of what Washington County place-name?

A. Ochelata.

Q. What town is the home of East Central Oklahoma State University?

A. Ada.

Q. In the 1890s, Cleveland had the only bridge across the Arkansas River between Tulsa and the Kansas line, which earned the town what title?

A. "Gate City."

Q. The Greek goddess of harvest is the namesake of what Noble County community?

A. Ceres.

Q. From what natural feature did Stillwater draw its name?

A. Stillwater Creek.

Q. Marietta is the seat of what county?

A. Love.

Q. The place-name Wetumka has what meaning in the Creek language?

A. "Noisy waters," or "sounding waters."

Q. A onetime tailor at Fort Sill and later a trader in the Chickasaw Nation is the namesake of what Stephens County town?

A. Duncan (for William Duncan).

Q. In what town is Oklahoma Panhandle State University?

A. Goodwell.

Q. Before the coming of the railroad in 1892, Comanche was known by what name?

A. Wilson Town.

Q. Although Cordell today holds the title, what was the original seat of Washita County?

A. Cloud Chief.

Q. What Kiowa County town is named for a past vice president of the United States, who served from 1897 to 1899?

A. Hobart (for Garrett A. Hobart).

Q. Texawa is the former name of what Tillman County town?

A. Davidson.

Q. What now-vanished community founded by Wyandotte Indian entrepreneur Mathias Splitlog was the first town in Delaware County?

A. Cayuga.

Q. Drumright was first known by what name?

A. Fulkerson.

Q. A nephew of Confederate General Stand Watie is the namesake of what Delaware County town?

A. Jay (for Jay Washburn).

Q. By what prior name was Brinkman in Greer County known?

A. Kell.

Q. What is the seat of Alfalfa County?

A. Cherokee.

Q. For what Osage leader was Pawhuska named?

A. Chief Pahu-çka (or "White Hair").

Q. Where is Cameron University?

A. Lawton.

Q. The French trader's term *salaison*, meaning "salt provisions," or "salt meat," became the basis for what town's name?

A. Sallisaw.

Q. Although Shawnee prevailed, what sister town bitterly fought to become the seat of Pottawatomie County in the 1890s?

A. Tecumseh.

Q. What Rogers County community was named in honor of the chief of the Cherokee Nation from 1879 to 1887?

A. Bushyhead (for Dennis W. Bushyhead).

Q. From where were the majority of settlers who staked lands that became the town of Stillwater?

A. Cowley County, Kansas.

Q. By what name was the 1886 railroad siding known from which Waynoka eventually developed?

A. Keystone.

Q. Edmond is the home of what university?

A. Central State.

Q. When founded, what was the largest Mennonite community in the state?

A. Meno.

Q. Elk City derived its name from what local natural feature?

A. Elk Creek.

———ɷɷɷ———

Q. What is the largest county in the state?

A. Osage.

———ɷɷɷ———

Q. A stand of trees encircling what Major County community gave the town its name when platted in 1901?

A. Ringwood.

———ɷɷɷ———

Q. Where is Oklahoma Baptist University?

A. Shawnee.

———ɷɷɷ———

Q. A group of Southern Methodists founded what Lincoln County town in 1903?

A. Davenport.

———ɷɷɷ———

Q. What was the original name of Taft?

A. Twine (for W. H. Twine).

———ɷɷɷ———

Q. From where in 1850 did Creek Indian Jim Sapulpa, for whom Sapulpa is named, relocate to settle on Rock Creek?

A. Alabama.

Q. What is the seat of Canadian County?

A. El Reno.

Q. When first officially added to Oklahoma, the entire Panhandle was designated as what county?

A. Beaver.

Q. What town, when platted in 1893, was named by subchief of the Cheyennes, Mon-On-Cloud?

A. Waynoka.

Q. What Cimarron County town site was laid out by a nephew of P. T. Barnum in 1892?

A. Kenton.

Q. In 1903, what all-black community was founded in Okfuskee County?

A. Boley.

Q. For what onetime murder defendant, and later sheriff of the Flint District of the Cherokee Nation, was Proctor named?

A. Ezekal Proctor.

Q. What is the seat of Grady County?

A. Chickasha.

Q. The capital of Czechoslovakia is the namesake of what Lincoln County town?

A. Prague.

Q. Fairland evolved from what prior community some two and one-half miles east of its present location?

A. Prairie City.

Q. Prior to receiving its present official name from the post office, Seminole was known by what name?

A. Tidmore.

ENTERTAINMENT

C H A P T E R   T W O

Q. What nickname did Will Rogers receive early in his career, while working in wild west shows?

A. "The Cherokee Kid."

—◇◇◇—

Q. On the flip of a coin, what Clearmore-born guitar player lost his seat on the ill-fated airplane flight that took the lives of early rock 'n' roll legends Ritchie Valens, Buddy Holly, and the Big Bopper (Jiles P. Richardson)?

A. Tommy Allsup.

—◇◇◇—

Q. What native of Oklahoma produced and directed the hilarious *Pink Panther* movie series?

A. Blake Edwards.

—◇◇◇—

Q. Prior to pursuing an acting career, Tom Mix served as deputy town marshal in what community in 1912?

A. Dewey.

—◇◇◇—

Q. What Clayton-born musician was the original piano player for the nationally known country and gospel group The Plainsmen?

A. Easmon Napier.

Q. What Hugo cemetery features an area called "Showman's Rest," where many circus performers and employees are interred?

A. Mt. Olive Cemetery.

Q. For what series did Oklahoma-born television producer Doug Benton receive an Emmy in 1974?

A. *Columbo.*

Q. Where was actor Ben Johnson born on June 13, 1918?

A. Foreacre.

Q. What 1970 song with an Oklahoma theme was a country hit for Merle Haggard?

A. "Okie From Muskogee."

Q. Where was the boyhood home of black screen character actor Stepin Fetchit (Lincoln Perry)?

A. Gowen.

Q. In 1978, what song with Tulsa in its title became a hit single for country artist Don Williams?

A. "Tulsa Time (Living On Tulsa Time)."

Q. Kingfisher was the hometown of what silent film actor who appeared in 55 movies?

A. Jack Hoxie.

Q. Who was billed in his early radio career as "Oklahoma's Yodeling Cowboy"?

A. Gene Autry.

Q. Known for his many western-themed roles, what actor of both television and the silver screen was born in Oklahoma City in 1923?

A. Dale Robertson.

Q. In what 1957 movie did Tulsa-born Tony Randall make his screen debut?

A. *Oh Men! Oh Women!*

Q. What Erick-born actor/singer/songwriter costarred in the long-running television series *Rawhide* as the character Pete Nolan?

A. Sheb Wooley.

Q. Where was country-and-western singer/songwriter Floyd Tillman born on December 8, 1914?

A. Ryan.

Q. In 1994, what Tulsa-based group burst on the progressive country music scene with a self-titled debut album?

A. The Tractors.

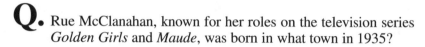

Q. Rue McClanahan, known for her roles on the television series *Golden Girls* and *Maude*, was born in what town in 1935?

A. Healdton.

Q. What somewhat enigmatic rocker, who made the 1972 gold album *Carney*, was born in Lawton on April 2, 1941?

A. Leon Russell.

Q. What University of Oklahoma graduate appeared in such films as *The Strange One, Splendor in the Grass,* and *Cool Hand Luke*?

A. Lou Antonio.

Q. On March 28, 1954, what world-famous female country artist was born at Chockie?

A. Reba McEntire.

Q. What group, which originated in Oklahoma City in 1983, has created such singles as "In A Priest Driven Ambulance," "Hit to Death in The Future Head," and "She Don't Use Jelly"?

A. Flaming Lips.

Q. A large wooden roller coaster, log ride, and skyride are all part of what Tulsa attraction?

A. Bell's Amusement Park.

Q. What Oklahoma-raised singer/songwriter composed the theme song for and narrated Walt Disney's animated classic *Robin Hood*?

A. Roger Miller.

Q. In late 1994, what Oklahoman came to national attention with his hit country single, "When The Wrong One Loves You Right"?

A. Wade Hayes.

Q. What native of Grand was known as the "King of Western Swing"?

A. Donell C. "Spade" Cooley.

Q. Where was actress Alice Ghostley born and raised?

A. Henryetta.

Q. What Norman-born actor is best known for his hit television series *Maverick* and *Rockford Files*?

A. James Garner.

Q. With whom did Tulsan Ronnie Dunn team up for the 1991 album *Brand New Man*, which launched one of country music's all-time most popular duos?

A. Kix Brooks.

———⬡⬡⬡———

Q. Where is the Jerry Kirk Memorial Fiddlers Convention held?

A. Elk City.

———⬡⬡⬡———

Q. What Oklahoma City native was best known for his title role in the ABC radio series *Pat Novak for Hire*?

A. Ben Morris

———⬡⬡⬡———

Q. What Oklahoman is known for his roles in *A River Runs Through It, Twelve Monkeys,* and *Legends of the Fall*?

A. Brad Pitt.

———⬡⬡⬡———

Q. Native Oklahoman and University of Tulsa graduate Matthew Mungle received an Oscar for his makeup artistry on what horror movie?

A. *Bram Stoker's Dracula.*

———⬡⬡⬡———

Q. What was the actual name of Pawnee Bill, who gained world fame with his Pawnee Bill's Wild West Circus?

A. Major Gordon E. Little.

Q. In 1958, what western-styled theme park opened on the northeastern side of Oklahoma City?

A. Frontier City Theme Park.

———∞∞∞———

Q. What R&B trio, comprised of brothers Charles, Ronnie, and Robert Wilson, derived its name from the nickname of the area around the three Tulsa streets Greenwood, Archer, and Pine?

A. The Gap Band.

———∞∞∞———

Q. What is the hometown of country superstar Garth Brooks?

A. Yukon.

———∞∞∞———

Q. What star of the silver screen was at one time a photographer in Lawton?

A. Lon Chaney, Jr.

———∞∞∞———

Q. Annually drawing thousands of gospel music fans, what town has hosted the Oklahoma All-Night Gospel Singing since the early 1960s?

A. Konawa.

———∞∞∞———

Q. What 1973 motion picture, starring Faye Dunaway, dealt with oil wildcatting in 1913 Oklahoma?

A. *Oklahoma Crude.*

Q. Where was country artist Bryan White born on February 17, 1974?

A. Lawton.

Q. What annual event at Cushing features some of Oklahoma's best blues bands?

A. Bar-B-Q 'n' Blues Festival.

Q. Okema is the birthplace of what activist folk singer of the dust bowl era?

A. Woodrow Wilson "Woody" Guthrie.

Q. What Stillwater native appeared in the *Blossom* and *Party of Five* television series?

A. Jimmy Marsden.

Q. Chief Thundercloud (Victor Daniels), who appeared in 62 movies in the 1930s, 40s, and 50s, was born in what town in 1889?

A. Muskogee.

Q. What country singer from Oklahoma became a leader in his field during the 1990s with such hit singles as "Home," "Bigger Than The Beatles," "Pickup Man," and "John Deere Green"?

A. Joe Diffie.

Q. Where is the Country Western Hall of Fame?

A. Del City.

———∞∞∞———

Q. What jazz trumpeter and singer was born in Yale on December 23, 1929?

A. Chesney Henry "Chet" Baker.

———∞∞∞———

Q. What director/producer born in Oklahoma City on August 21, 1901, had over 2,000 films to his credit?

A. Albert S. Rogell.

———∞∞∞———

Q. In 1919, what actress was born Phyllis Isley in Tulsa?

A. Jennifer Jones.

———∞∞∞———

Q. What country artist was born Patricia Gail Dickerson in 1946 at Broken Bow?

A. Gail Davies.

———∞∞∞———

Q. Billed as the oldest bluegrass festival west of the Mississippi, where is the Grant's Blue Grass Music Festival held each August?

A. Salt Creek Park, Hugo.

———∞∞∞———

Q. In the fall of 1991, what Garth Brooks recording project became the third country album in history to reach the top spot on Billboard's pop music charts?

A. *Ropin' the Wind.*

Q. Ranked as one of the all-time greatest blues guitarists, where was Wayne Bennett born in 1933?

A. Sulphur.

———— ∞∞ ————

Q. What actress from Norman played the role of Dr. Carol Novins on the television series *St. Elsewhere*?

A. Cindy Pickett.

———— ∞∞ ————

Q. Where was country superstar Vincent Grant "Vince" Gill born on April 12, 1957?

A. Norman.

———— ∞∞ ————

Q. On what television series did Hoyt Axton make his acting debut in 1962?

A. *Bonanza*.

———— ∞∞ ————

Q. Oklahoma City is the hometown of what actor who appeared in the motion pictures *Hamburger Hill* and *Biloxi Blues*?

A. Michael Dolan.

———— ∞∞ ————

Q. What Tulsa-born R&B bandleader during the 1950s created the great hit singles "Flamingo," "Sleep," "You Go To My Head," "Cherokee," and "Temptation"?

A. Earl Bostic.

Q. Child star Darla Hood, who played the role of "Darla" in the popular *Our Gang* series, was born in what town?

A. Leedey.

———⟨∞⟩———

Q. What character did Tulsa-born actor Larry Drake play on the television series L. A. Law?

A. Benny Stulwicz.

———⟨∞⟩———

Q. Motion picture director Jerry Hopper, who directed *Hurricane Smith, The Secret of the Incas, Naked Alibi,* and *The Private War of Major Benson,* was born in what Oklahoma town in 1907?

A. Guthrie.

———⟨∞⟩———

Q. What Oklahoma City–born jazz tenor saxophonist toured with the Earl Hines Band from 1943 to 1945?

A. Wardell Gray.

———⟨∞⟩———

Q. While in high school, what was the name of Vince Gill's bluegrass band?

A. Mountain Smoke.

———⟨∞⟩———

Q. What 1981 Miss America from Elk City hosted the television show *Home Matters*?

A. Susan Powell.

Q. Oklahoma City natives Bryan Abrams, Mark Calderon, Sam Watters, and Kevin "KT" Thornton formed what R&B revival group in 1987?

A. Color Me Bad.

Q. Tulsa is the hometown of what actor/comic who appeared in *Mississippi Burning* and *Fried Green Tomatoes*?

A. Gailard Sartain.

Q. From spring until winter, what Guthrie attraction presents musical comedy, ragtime piano, and banjo?

A. Presentation Playhouse.

Q. Muskogee was the hometown of what electric jazz guitarist who worked with Artie Shaw's Gramercy Five, Charlie Parker, and The Oscar Peterson Trio?

A. Barney Kessel.

Q. What co-host of the popular prime-time television series *Laugh-In* was from Beggs?

A. Dan Rowan.

Q. Among the musicians that comprised the group Tweed, what three members were born in Tulsa?

A. Wendell Harrold, Rick Gomez, and Jimmy Thomas Ray.

Q. What silent film star, who appeared in some 90 films between 1910 and 1929, was born in Stillwater?

A. Art Acord.

Q. Pauls Valley–born Jean Shepard teamed with Ferlin Husky on what top country single on Capitol Records?

A. "Dear John Letter."

Q. What Oklahoma character actor appeared in the now-classic television series *Our Miss Brooks* and *The Ann Sothern Show*?

A. Don Porter.

Q. Where was pop singer and actress Patti Page born on November 8, 1927?

A. Claremore.

Q. Oklahoma City is the hometown of what actor who appeared in the *Knott's Landing* and *Dallas* television series?

A. Ted Shackelford.

Q. What Sheb Wooley comic alter ego won the Country Music Association's Comedian of The Year award in 1968?

A. Ben Colder.

Q. What Native-American actor from Oklahoma appeared in such motion pictures as *One Flew Over the Cuckoo's Nest, Standing Tall,* and *Firewalker?*

A. Will Sampson.

———— ∞∞∞ ————

Q. Michael Dunn, who was born in Shattuck, received a best supporting actor Oscar nomination in 1966 for his role in what motion picture?

A. *Ship of Fools.*

———— ∞∞∞ ————

Q. What Muskogee-born jazz pianist, also known for his blues and boogie-woogie style, helped develop the jazz tradition of Kansas City?

A. James Columbus "Jay" McShann.

———— ∞∞∞ ————

Q. Wes Studi, who appeared in the motion pictures *Dances with Wolves* and *Geronimo*, hails from what small Oklahoma town?

A. Nofire Hollow.

———— ∞∞∞ ————

Q. Cowboy movie star Sunset Carson, who appeared in westerns from 1943 to 1950, was born in what town?

A. Gracemont.

———— ∞∞∞ ————

Q. What was Lon Chaney, Jr., named when he was born in Oklahoma City on February 10, 1906?

A. Creighton Tull Chaney.

Q. During his long career, what character actor from Oklahoma appeared in over 220 films?

A. Frank Ellis.

Q. What Oklahoma City jazz band of the 1920s was led by bassist Walter Page?

A. The Blue Devils.

Q. Oklahoma City native H. Gray Frederickson, Jr., was executive producer for what epic Vietnam War movie?

A. *Apocalypse Now.*

Q. What was Dale Robertson's first television western series?

A. *Wells Fargo.*

Q. Featuring live country-and-western music, where is the Oklahoma Opry?

A. Oklahoma City.

Q. What actress from Boise City appeared in such movies as *Jubilee Trail, Psycho, The Man Who Shot Liberty Valance,* and *Sergeant Ryker*?

A. Vera Miles.

Q. On what ranch just north of present-day Oologah was Will Rogers born on November 4, 1879?

A. Dog Iron Ranch.

———————

Q. What Oklahoma City–born film editor/director/producer has such memorable movies to his credit as *20,000 Leagues Under The Sea; The Longest Day; Tora! Tora! Tora!; Those Magnificent Men in Their Flying Machines; The Blue Max;* and *Zorba the Greek*?

A. Elmo Williams.

———————

Q. Armina Marshall, who was born in Alfalfa County in 1899, received a Tony in 1958 as co-producer of what theatrical work?

A. *Sunrise at Campobello.*

———————

Q. What western swing artist was known for his Tulsa Stampede?

A. Johnnie Lee Wills.

———————

Q. In 1944, Universal Studios released what Oklahoma-themed western starring Tex Ritter?

A. *Oklahoma Raiders.*

———————

Q. Where was actress Barbara Lawrence born on February 24, 1930?

A. Carnegie.

Q. What actor, born in Ryan on March 10, 1940, is known for the martial arts movies *Return of the Dragon, Force of One,* and *The Delta Force?*

A. Carlos Ray "Chuck" Norris.

━━━∞∞∞━━━

Q. The role of Emmett Ryker in the television series *The Virginian* was played by what actor from Holdenville?

A. Clu Gulager.

━━━∞∞∞━━━

Q. What supporting actor from Oklahoma City appeared in such films as *The China Syndrome* and *Hanger 18* and the television series *F-Troop?*

A. James Hampton.

━━━∞∞∞━━━

Q. In 1959, country artist Sheb Wooley spent six weeks at the top of the pop charts with what self-penned single?

A. "Purple People Eater."

━━━∞∞∞━━━

Q. Warner Brothers released what Oklahoma-themed movie starring James Cagney and Humphrey Bogart in 1939?

A. *Oklahoma Kid.*

━━━∞∞∞━━━

Q. What Tulsan played the recurring role of Nancy Thompson in the *Nightmare on Elm Street* horror film series?

A. Heather Langenkamp.

Q. Actress Glenda Farrell, who appeared in some 75 movies, was born in what town in 1904?

A. Enid.

———❈———

Q. What is Clinton-born country artist Toby Keith's actual last name?

A. Covel.

———❈———

Q. Cowboy star Johnny Mack Brown appeared in what 1951 Monogram motion picture with an Oklahoma theme?

A. *Oklahoma Justice.*

———❈———

Q. In mid-1976, what became Reba McEntire's first charting single?

A. "I Don't Want to Be a One Night Stand."

———❈———

Q. *The Firm* and *Waterworld* are among the acting credits of what actress born in Tulsa in 1975?

A. Jeanne Tripplehorn.

———❈———

Q. What character did Alice Ghostley play in the television series *Designing Women*?

A. Bernice.

———❈———

Q. In 1981, what country song with Oklahoma in its title became a huge hit single for the duo of David Frizzell and Shelly West?

A. "You're the Reason God Made Oklahoma."

Q. William Witney, who directed some 92 films between 1937 and 1975, was born in what town on May 15, 1910?

A. Lawton.

───❀───

Q. For what movie did Ben Johnson receive an Oscar in 1971?

A. *The Last Picture Show.*

───❀───

Q. In a first-time-ever event, where did an ensemble of 100 pianos perform live over CBS radio in 1934?

A. Tulsa.

───❀───

Q. What actor born in Oklahoma Territory in 1901, in addition to appearing in over 140 films, played the role of Sheriff Blodgett on the *Roy Rogers* television series?

A. Harry Harvey.

───❀───

Q. What Fort Sill native played the role of Mother Dexter on the television series *Phyllis*?

A. Judith Lowry.

───❀───

Q. What country singer/actress, who was born in Oklahoma City on August 18, 1939, appeared in *Summer Love, Going Steady,* and *Chartroose Caboose*?

A. Molly Bee.

Q. The affiliation of what two circuses with Hugo earned the town the nickname of "Circus City USA"?

A. Carson and Barnes Circus and Kelley-Miller Circus.

Q. What two western swing entertainers composed the classic "Take Me Back to Tulsa"?

A. Bob Wills and Tommy Duncan.

Q. Known for such televisions series as *Dr. Kildare, The Girl from UNCLE, Columbo, Ironside, The Rookies,* and *Police Woman,* where was producer Doug Benton born on September 24, 1925?

A. Hollis.

Q. What native Oklahoman appeared in the motion picture *Darkman*?

A. Larry Drake.

Q. Who played the role of Woody Guthrie in the 1976 film based on Guthrie's autobiography *Bound for Glory*?

A. David Carradine.

Q. Where was actor Cleavon Little born on June 1, 1939?

A. Chickasha.

Q. What Tulsan appeared in the motion pictures *Miss Firecracker, Crooklyn,* and *Star Trek: First Contact*?

A. Alfre Woodard.

Q. Where was the Blackhawk Blues Band formed in 1990?

A. Oklahoma City.

Q. What Oklahoma City native served as executive producer on the *Bring'em Back Alive* television series?

A. Jay Bernstein.

Q. What former Miss Oklahoma was born in Barnsdall on March 25, 1940?

A. Anita Bryant.

Q. In 1974, what Oklahoma City–born producer received an Oscar for *The Godfather Part II*?

A. H. Gray Frederickson, Jr.

Q. What Dewey resident became the third wife of cowboy star Tom Mix?

A. Olive Stokes.

Q. What Norman-born actress appeared in such motion pictures as *American Graffiti, The Man Who Fell to Earth, Johnny Belinda,* and *The Big Sleep*?

A. Candy Clark.

Q. Highly versatile performer Sheb Wooley, who was born in Erick on April 10, 1921, played what whiskey-drinking killer in the classic western motion picture *High Noon*?

A. Ben Miller.

Q. Suzy Amis, who has appeared in the movies *Cadillac Ranch* and *The Usual Suspects*, was born in what town on January 5, 1958?

A. Oklahoma City.

Q. Who is credited with suggesting that Gene Autry pursue a singing career on radio?

A. Will Rogers.

Q. What Oklahoma City actress played the role of Mona Kane on the soap opera *All My Children* from 1970 to 1994?

A. Frances Heflin.

Q. Where was motion picture and television producer, director, and writer, Blake Edwards, born on July 26, 1922?

A. Tulsa.

Q. What famous radio and television newscaster was born in Ada?

A. Douglas Edwards.

Q. Known as one of the premier gospel music events in the state, the annual Seminole Gospel Sing began in what year?

A. 1971.

Q. What Duncan-born actor/singer/songwriter, appeared in *E.T., The Black Stallion, Gremlins,* and *We're No Angels*?

A. Hoyt Axton.

Q. Walters-born actor Van Heflin received an Oscar for best supporting actor in what 1942 motion picture?

A. *Johnny Eager.*

Q. Where is the Tom Mix Museum and Western Theater?

A. Dewey.

Q. What native of Mangum appeared in some 25 movies including *White Man's Burden, Magnum Force,* and *The Color Purple*?

A. Margaret Avery.

Q. Garth Brooks' mother, Colleen, starred on what 1950s national country music television show?

A. *Ozark Mountain Jubilee.*

Q. What singer/songwriter/guitarist, born and raised in Oklahoma, released his debut solo album, *On the Verge of a Nervous Breakthrough*, in 1994 on Quincy Jones's Qwest Records?

A. Michael Been.

Q. Haskell is the hometown of what actor who played the role of "Whitey" in some 25 *Bowery Boys* films?

A. William "Billy" Benedict.

Q. What rock band, founded in Oklahoma City in the early 1990s, had their single "Slip Slide Melting" selected as part of the soundtrack for the motion picture *The Crow*?

A. For Love Not Lisa.

Q. What Tulsa water park offers two 75-foot speed slides?

A. Big Splash Water Park.

Q. What Tulsa-born guitarist and vocalist in the 1960s was a founding member of the Paul Butterfield Blues Band?

A. Elvin Bishop.

Q. For her role in what motion picture did Jennifer Jones receive an Oscar?

A. *The Song of Bernadette* (1944).

Q. In what west Oklahoma town was multi-talented country/pop artist Roger Miller raised by his uncle?

A. Erick.

Q. What Oklahoman directed the television series *Kung Fu*?

A. Jerry Hopper.

Q. In 1944, where was folk rocker Mike Brewer, who had the 1971 hit single "One Toke Over The Line," born?

A. Oklahoma City.

Q. What motion picture studio created *Oklahoma Renegades, The Tulsa Kid, Oklahoma Badlands,* and *Oklahoma Annie*?

A. Republic Pictures.

Q. Although born in Goose Creek, Texas, what actor, who starred in the motion picture *The Buddy Holly Story*, lived for a time in both Tulsa and Stillwater?

A. Gary Busey.

Q. What Oklahoman stars in the television series *Walker, Texas Ranger*?

A. Chuck Norris.

Q. During the 1990s, what Broken Bow resident garnered eight number one country/Christian hit singles?

A. Judy DeRamus.

Q. Tulsa-born musician David Gates co-founded what group in 1968?

A. Bread.

Q. What wild west show, originating from Kay County, became internationally famous in the decade just prior to World War I?

A. The Miller Brother's 101 Wild West Show.

Q. Where was country-and-western singer Norma Jean born on January 30, 1938?

A. Wellston.

Q. What Oklahoma-born actress appeared in *Captain from Castile, Give My Regards to Broadway, Oklahoma,* and *Joe Dakota*?

A. Barbara Lawrence.

Q. Where was actor Brad Pitt born on December 18, 1963?

A. Shawnee.

Q. In what town, on September 25, 1898, did Ringling Brothers Circus set an attendance record under a single tent with some 30,000 paid admissions?

A. Enid.

Q. Where is the National Four String Banjo Hall of Fame Museum?

A. Guthrie.

Q. What Tulsa-based group burst on the teen-pop scene in the late 1990s with their smash hit single "MMMBop"?

A. Hanson.

Q. Early in her professional singing career, Patti Page was a staff performer at what Tulsa radio station?

A. KTUL.

Q. What Oklahoma-born country singer is known for the singles "Should've Asked Her Faster," "Smoke in Her Eyes," "Redneck Son," "Irresistible You," and "All of the Above"?

A. Ty England.

Q. The motion pictures *Bleep* and *The Brothers O'Toole* were directed by what native of Enid?

A. Richard Erdman.

Q. What Texas-born jazz guitarist grew up in Oklahoma City and played with Benny Goodman from 1939 to 1941?

A. Charlie Christian.

Q. What was Sunset Carson's actual name?

A. Winifred Harrison.

Q. Although first performed on Broadway in 1943, in what year was the motion picture version of the musical *Oklahoma!* released?

A. 1955.

Q. In 1894, what Oklahoma entertainment extravaganza performed at the World's Fair in Antwerp, Belgium?

A. Pawnee Bill's Wild West Circus.

Q. Buried in Hugo's Mt. Olive Cemetery, who was the original "Buster Brown" of Buster Brown Shoes fame?

A. William Edmond Ansley.

Q. *The Man Who Loved Cat Dancing, The Longest Yard, W. W. and the Dixie Dance Kings, The China Syndrome*, and *Condorman* are among the screen credits of what Oklahoma City–born actor?

A. James Hampton.

Q. Prior to pursuing a career in music, where did Gene Autry work as a telegraph operator?

A. Sapulpa.

Q. For his editing work on what classic western motion picture did Oklahoma City native Elmo Williams receive an Oscar in 1952?

A. *High Noon.*

Q. In 1945, what self-penned tune became Spade Cooley's biggest hit record?

A. "Shame On You."

Q. What Oklahoman played Esmerelda on the television series *Bewitched*?

A. Alice Ghostley.

Q. Rochelle Hudson, who appeared in *Rebel Without a Cause, Poppy,* and *Born Reckless*, was a native of what town?

A. Oklahoma City.

Q. Where was Native-American actor Iron Eyes Cody born on April 3, 1915?

A. Tulsa.

Q. What University of Oklahoma graduate produced *The Man Who Wouldn't Die; The Good, the Bad, and the Ugly; Little Fauss and Big Halsey;* and *The Godfather*?

A. H. Gray Frederickson, Jr.

Q. For what television series did Tony Randall receive an Emmy in 1975?

A. *The Odd Couple.*

Q. What Shidler native made his big screen debut in the original version of the motion picture *Mighty Joe Young*?

A. Ben Johnson.

Q. Where is the Memorial Weekend Jazz and Blues Festival held?

A. Edmond.

Q. What Oklahoman was replaced on the nationally syndicated *Porter Wagoner Show* in the mid-1960s by Dolly Parton?

A. Norma Jean.

Q. What Oklahoma actor appeared in *Blazing Saddles* and *Once Bitten*?

A. Cleavon Little.

Q. Singer Wanda Jackson, whose musical offerings have spanned country, rockabilly, and gospel, was born in what town in 1937?

A. Maud.

Q. What Oklahoma-born actor starred in such television series as *The Iron Horse, Death Valley Days, Dynasty,* and *J. J. Starbuck*?

A. Dale Robertson.

Q. What was Patti Page's birth name?

A. Clara Ann Flower.

HISTORY

Q. What Roaring Twenties benefactor to Ponca City was known as "Daddy Long Legs"?

A. Lew Wentz.

———⊗⊗⊗———

Q. The attic room of the Stuart Hotel was used as an occasional hideout for what 1930s desperado?

A. Charles Arthur "Pretty Boy" Floyd.

———⊗⊗⊗———

Q. On what date did Oklahoma become the 46th state in the Union?

A. November 16, 1907.

———⊗⊗⊗———

Q. In a mass town meeting on May 23, 1889, who was chosen to become the first provisional mayor of Oklahoma City?

A. William L. Couch.

———⊗⊗⊗———

Q. Where did William Wrigley manufacture his first package of chewing gum?

A. Guthrie (113 North Division Street).

Q. In the 1920s, what Oklahoma town had more millionaires per capita than New York City?

A. Okmulgee.

Q. Over a 35-year span, what black deputy marshal, appointed to patrol Indian Territory by "hanging" Judge Parker, brought to justice over 3,000 outlaws?

A. Bass Reeves.

Q. Upon the selection of Oklahoma City as the state capital in 1910, Governor Charles Haskell declared what Oklahoma City hostelry as the temporary capitol?

A. Lee-Huckins Hotel.

Q. Into what two sections was the legislative branch of the Creek (Muscogee) Nation divided?

A. House of Kings and House of Warriors.

Q. In 1541, what Spanish explorer crossed the western portion of present-day Oklahoma?

A. Francisco Vásquez de Coronado.

Q. Following the incorporation of Tulsa as a town on January 18, 1898, who was elected the city's first mayor?

A. Colonel Edward Colkins.

Q. Between noon and sunset on April 22, 1889, how many settlers flocked into the new town of Oklahoma City?

A. Some 10,000.

———∞∞∞———

Q. In 1880, what institution of higher learning was founded in Muskogee with help from the American Baptist Churches, U.S.A.?

A. Bacone College.

———∞∞∞———

Q. What son of the 9th governor became the state's 14th governor in 1951?

A. Johnston Murray (son of William H. Murray).

———∞∞∞———

Q. Who opened a trading post in 1796 near the site of present-day Salina?

A. Pierre Chonteau.

———∞∞∞———

Q. What name was given to would-be-settlers led by C. C. Carpenter, David L. Payne, and William L. Couch, who pressed the federal government to open Indian lands for settlement by whites?

A. "Boomers."

———∞∞∞———

Q. According to the 1890 Federal census, what was the population of the Five Civilized Tribes?

A. 50,055.

Q. During 1886 and 1887, what railroad company laid track from north to south through the Indian Territory?

A. Atchison, Topeka, and Santa Fe Railroad.

Q. What World War II submarine is on display in Muskogee?

A. USS *Batfish.*

Q. In 1848, what prominent Creek rancher opened the first trading post near the Lochapoka settlement on the site of present-day Tulsa?

A. Lewis Perryman.

Q. What one-time candidate for president of the United States on the Populist ticket attempted but failed to be selected as the first provisional mayor of Oklahoma City?

A. James B. Weaver.

Q. What Kiowa leader was known as the "Orator of the Plains"?

A. Satanta.

Q. The first fire station in Indian Territory, a small log structure to house a hand-drawn hose cart, was constructed where in 1869?

A. Fort Supply.

Q. Who created the Creek Indian Memorial Association in 1923 to preserve Creek (Muscogee) culture?

A. Judge Orlando B. Swain.

———— ∞ ————

Q. From 1682 to 1762 and 1800 to 1803, what European nation claimed lands which included present-day Oklahoma?

A. France.

———— ∞ ————

Q. In 1879, what famous chief, along with fellow Nez Percé Indians, was relocated to the Salt Fork of the Arkansas River near present-day Tonkawa?

A. Chief Joseph.

———— ∞ ————

Q. What Ponca City 1920s oil tycoon's adopted daughter, Lydie, became his second wife?

A. E. W. Marland.

———— ∞ ————

Q. Consisting of 400 city blocks and some 2,169 structures, where is the largest urban historic district listed on the National Register of Historic Places?

A. Guthrie.

———— ∞ ————

Q. Broadcasting from Oklahoma City in 1921, what was Oklahoma's first radio station?

A. WKY.

Q. The First Regiment of Oklahoma's National Guard saw action in Mexico against what rebel leader in 1916?

A. Pancho Villa.

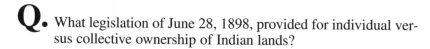

Q. What legislation of June 28, 1898, provided for individual versus collective ownership of Indian lands?

A. The Curtis Act.

Q. What organization established the Five Civilized Tribes Museum in the 1950s?

A. Da-Co-Tah Indian Club.

Q. Who was the last Osage chief to receive a traditional burial, complete with the killing of his horse and the placing of a human scalp on his grave?

A. Chief Ne-ka-wa-she-tun-ka.

Q. Developing his wealth from a chain of twenty-eight trading posts across Indian Territory, who became the first millionaire in the Choctaw Nation?

A. Robert M. Jones.

Q. In 1963, who became the state's first Republican governor?

A. Henry Bellmon.

Q. During what Civil War battle, fought near present-day Muskogee, did black soldiers first fight alongside white troops?

A. Battle of Honey Springs.

———∞∞∞———

Q. In 1858, on Little Creek in what is present-day Ellis County, what Comanche warrior chief, known for wearing an old coat of Spanish mail into battle, was killed in a shoot-out with Texas Rangers?

A. Prohebits Quasho (Iron Jacket).

———∞∞∞———

Q. What noted Comanche chief rode at the head of his people when they surrendered to military authorities at Fort Sill in 1875?

A. Quanah Parker.

———∞∞∞———

Q. Started in 1949 and completed in 1953, what was the state's first turnpike?

A. Turner Turnpike (Oklahoma City to Tulsa).

———∞∞∞———

Q. Where did East and West Cherokees meet in 1839 to sign the Act of Union?

A. Takotokah (northwest of present-day Tahlequah).

———∞∞∞———

Q. Who was the first and only black physician in Eufaula from 1908 to the mid-1930s?

A. Dr. C. L. Cooper.

Q. In 1882, what two coal miners from Illinois established the first labor union in Indian Territory?

A. Dill Carroll and Frank Murphy.

Q. What notorious Apache chief was sent to Fort Sill in 1894, where he remained under military supervision until his death in 1909?

A. Geronimo.

Q. Although the state flag was officially adopted on April 2, 1925, what was added to the design in 1940?

A. The word *Oklahoma*.

Q. By 1920, what city was the "Oil Capital of the World"?

A. Tulsa.

Q. Under 1876 federal law, where was the first marriage license issued in Indian Territory?

A. Muscogee (Muskogee).

Q. What Oklahoma Choctaw received the Croix de Guerre from French Marshal Pétain for single-handedly capturing 171 enemy troops during World War I?

A. Private Joseph Oklahombi.

Q. Under what name was Stillwater's Oklahoma State University opened in the 1890s?

A. Oklahoma Agricultural and Mechanical College.

———∞∞∞———

Q. What Creek leader did President William McKinley call the "greatest living Indian" of his time?

A. Chief Pleasant Porter.

———∞∞∞———

Q. In 1824, where was the first post office established within the borders of the present-day state?

A. Miller Courthouse.

———∞∞∞———

Q. Who served as president of the State Constitutional Convention and, 24 years later in 1931, became governor?

A. William H. "Alfalfa Bill" Murray.

———∞∞∞———

Q. Prior to being designated as Indian Territory, and later as Oklahoma Territory, the lands comprising the present-day state were included in what three other U.S. territories?

A. Louisiana, Missouri, and Arkansas.

———∞∞∞———

Q. Following the Civil War, what African-American town was founded west of Muskogee by former Creek slaves?

A. Taft.

Q. In 1829, by special act of the Cherokee Council in session at Tahlonteeskee on the Illinois River, what white man was formally adopted as a member of the tribe?

A. Sam Houston.

———∞∞∞———

Q. Who established a boatyard in 1819 in the Three Forks area near present-day Muskogee for the construction of keelboats?

A. Colonel Auguste Chouteau.

———∞∞∞———

Q. What nickname was given to Oklahomans who migrated to the West during the Great Depression?

A. "Okies."

———∞∞∞———

Q. In 1928, what Native-American health care facility was built at Claremore?

A. The United States Indian Hospital.

———∞∞∞———

Q. Due to the discovery of oil on their lands in the 1920s, members of what tribe were the richest race of people per capita in the world?

A. Osage.

———∞∞∞———

Q. What is the state motto?

A. "Labor Omnia Vincent" (Labor Conquers All).

Q. Who served as Oklahoma's first native-born governor from 1943–1947?

A. Robert S. Kerr.

Q. The Apache warrior chief, Geronimo, succumbed to what disease at Fort Sill on February 17, 1909?

A. Pneumonia.

Q. What tribe became the first to acquire relocation land in Oklahoma?

A. Choctaw.

Q. What soldier and statesman was elected Principal Chief of the Creek Nation in 1869, 1872, and 1879?

A. Samuel Checote.

Q. Following statehood in 1907, what did the first law passed by the new legislature establish?

A. Segregated public transportation.

Q. In 1834, what military facility was established by General Leavenworth at the present-day site of the Keystone Dam?

A. Fort Arbuckle.

Q. What Oklahoma World War II hero was honored by a guided missile frigate named in his honor?

A. Paul Henry Carr (the USS *Carr*).

Q. In 1893, under whose leadership did some 150 armed Choctaw Nationalists barricade themselves at Antlers, requiring the intervention of federal troops?

A. Victor M. Locke.

Q. What plasterer from Lawton organized a convention of labor union representatives that led to the formation of the Twin-Territorial Federation of Labor in 1903?

A. J. Harvey Lynch.

Q. Where is Sam Houston's Cherokee wife, Tiana Rogers, mis-inscribed as "Talihina" on her grave marker, interred?

A. Fort Gibson National Cemetery.

Q. In 1884, what religious organization established Tulsa's first mission school and church congregation?

A. Presbyterian Home Mission Board of New York City.

Q. What nickname applied to Oklahomans traces its origins back to the days of the great land runs?

A. "Sooners."

Q. What fort was established on the Little River near its juncture with the South Canadian River in 1834?

A. Fort Holmes.

———∞∞∞———

Q. In May 1909, where did Reverend John Mitchell organize the first Boy Scout troop in the United States?

A. Pawhuska.

———∞∞∞———

Q. To what tribe, in 1868, did the Cherokees sell the lands around present-day Nowata?

A. Kansas Delaware.

———∞∞∞———

Q. In 1922, what girls' organization was founded in McAlester by Reverend W. Mark Sexson under the sponsorship of the Order of the Eastern Star?

A. Order of the Rainbow.

———∞∞∞———

Q. Who established the 101 Ranch in 1879?

A. Colonel George Washington Miller.

———∞∞∞———

Q. In 1905, what African-American businessman relocated from Guthrie to Oklahoma City, where he developed his world-renowned East India Toilet Goods Company?

A. Sydney Lyons.

Q. What 1923 governor was impeached and removed from office after serving only nine months and fourteen days of his term?

A. John C. "Jack" Walton.

Q. In 1890, who became the first governor of Oklahoma Territory?

A. George Steele.

Q. Created to provide meals, cigarettes, writing paper, and hospitality to World War I soldiers traveling on troop trains, where was the first Red Cross canteen constructed in the United States?

A. El Reno.

Q. In 1866, what town became the capital of the Seminole in Indian Territory?

A. Wewoka.

Q. What was the original construction cost of the state capitol?

A. $1.5 million.

Q. In the early 1900s, what economically influential street in Tulsa became known as the "Black Wall Street"?

A. Greenwood Avenue.

Q. Who founded Fort Sill on January 8, 1869, during a winter campaign against Southern Plains tribes?

A. General Philip H. Sheridan.

———∞∞∞———

Q. In 1893, what town hosted delegates who drafted the first petition to the United States Congress for Oklahoma statehood?

A. Purcell.

———∞∞∞———

Q. What creator of the Cherokee alphabet settled near Sallisaw in the early 1800s?

A. Sequoyah (George Gist).

———∞∞∞———

Q. In 1837, what tribe surrendered their lands in the East and began relocation to Oklahoma?

A. Chickasaw.

———∞∞∞———

Q. The membership rolls of the Ku Klux Klan in Oklahoma soared to what figure in the 1920s?

A. Approximately 75,000.

———∞∞∞———

Q. In what year was Fort Gibson abandoned by the United States Army, only to be restored as a historical site in the 1930s?

A. 1890.

Q. How many acres comprised the Cherokee Outlet given by treaty to the Cherokee Nation for hunting grounds?

A. Over six million.

———

Q. Located at 6th and Denison and dating back to about 1903, what is the oldest black Protestant church in Muskogee?

A. First Baptist Church.

———

Q. Who did President Cleveland send to Fort Reno in 1874 to investigate Native-American unrest over grassland leases?

A. General Philip H. Sheridan.

———

Q. In 1929, who became Oklahoma's second governor to be removed from office through impeachment?

A. Henry S. Johnson.

———

Q. On April 6, 1934, a Miami constable was gunned down by what infamous couple?

A. Bonnie and Clyde (Bonnie Parker and Clyde Champion Barrow).

———

Q. In the worst case of domestic terrorism in U.S. history, how many lives were lost in the April 19, 1995, bombing of the Alfred P. Murrah Federal Building in Oklahoma City?

A. 168.

Q. Where were some 5,000 Creek Union loyalists bound for Kansas attacked by Confederate troops on November 19, 1861?

A. Round Mountain.

Q. What blacksmith was the first white resident of Okmulgee?

A. Silas Smith.

Q. By 1849, which tribe passed a law that forbade Blacks, either free or slave, from establishing towns in tribal lands?

A. Creek.

Q. For what was the 101 Ranch named?

A. Its cattle brand (101).

Q. In March 1897, the territorial legislature appropriated funds for the establishment of what center of higher education for African Americans?

A. Colored Agricultural and Normal University (now Langston University).

Q. What name was given the May 1872 shoot-out over Cherokee versus federal jurisdiction at a murder trial, which left seven law officers dead?

A. Goingsnake Massacre.

Q. What oil baron became the tenth governor of Oklahoma?

A. Ernest Whitworth Marland.

Q. In 1927, what Tulsan founded the U.S. Highway Route 66 Association to promote the Chicago to Los Angeles transportation artery?

A. Cyrus Avery.

Q. Where was the Oklahoma Historical Society organized in 1893?

A. Kingfisher.

Q. What Oklahoma native served as United States ambassador to the United Nations from 1981 to 1985?

A. Jeane Jordan Kirkpatrick.

Q. In the early1880s, where was the first federal jail constructed in Indian Territory?

A. Muskogee.

Q. Who selected Waynoka as the site of Oklahoma's first transcontinental airport in 1928?

A. Charles Lindbergh.

Q. In 1824, what fort was established at the confluence of the Arkansas, Verdigris, and Grand Rivers?

A. Fort Gibson.

Q. What McAlester-born attorney and politician served in the United States House of Representatives from 1946 to 1976?

A. Carl Albert.

———⟨⟩———

Q. The original 1892 staff of the University of Oklahoma consisted of how many instructors?

A. Four.

———⟨⟩———

Q. Members of the militant secret labor organization, the Working Class Union, were the driving force behind what 1917 uprising of some 2,000 farmers?

A. Green Corn Rebellion.

———⟨⟩———

Q. On June 23, 1865, who became the last Confederate general of the Civil War to surrender?

A. Brigadier General Stand Watie.

———⟨⟩———

Q. In 1907, what oil millionaire constructed a home for widows and orphans in what would become the town of Sand Springs?

A. Charles Page.

———⟨⟩———

Q. What future president spent several of his boyhood summers around Pawhuska with his uncle, Major Laban J. Miles, who was appointed the Osage agent in 1878?

A. Herbert Hoover.

Q. What federal legislation added the Panhandle area to Oklahoma Territory on May 2, 1890?

A. The Organic Act.

———∞∞∞———

Q. What was the first east-west railroad line to be established across the territory?

A. Atlantic and Pacific (which became the St. Louis and San Franciso).

———∞∞∞———

Q. What name did Native Americans give to the troopers of the 9th and 10th Cavalry?

A. Buffalo Soldiers.

———∞∞∞———

Q. In what year did the state's first television stations, Oklahoma City's KTVY and Tulsa's KOTV, begin broadcasting?

A. 1949.

———∞∞∞———

Q. What forerunner of TWA established a major terminal for its transcontinental air/rail service at Waynoka in the late 1920s?

A. TAT (Transcontinental Air Transportation).

———∞∞∞———

Q. For what per-acre price did the Cherokees sell the region known as the Cherokee Outlet to the federal government?

A. Approximately $1.40.

Q. What Woods County town was the site of a World War II P.O.W. camp with over 5,000 prisoners?

A. Alva.

———⟨⟩———

Q. When the Osage were relocated to Oklahoma in 1872, what amount was paid by the federal government as reimbursement for their lands in Kansas?

A. $9,000,000.

———⟨⟩———

Q. In 1990, Oklahoma became the first state to limit office terms of what public servants?

A. State legislators.

———⟨⟩———

Q. Due to his campaign in the 1920s for the construction of all-weather highways throughout the state, who became known as the "hard roads" governor?

A. Martin E. Trapp.

———⟨⟩———

Q. Where is noted aviator Wiley Post buried?

A. Edmond (Memorial Park Cemetery).

———⟨⟩———

Q. What church-related institute of higher learning opened its first classes in the fall of 1911?

A. Oklahoma Baptist University.

Q. What historic fort near Woodward originated in 1868 to accommodate the supply needs of Lt. Col. George A. Custer's winter campaign?

A. Fort Supply.

———— ∞∞ ————

Q. Ardmore came into being in 1877 on the land of what ranch owned by the Roff brothers?

A. 700 Ranch.

———— ∞∞ ————

Q. From where were the Pawnee relocated to the Pawnee Agency in 1876?

A. Nebraska.

———— ∞∞ ————

Q. What railroad line started laying track from Oklahoma City in 1890, and completed an east-west line across Indian and Oklahoma Territories from Arkansas to West Texas by 1904?

A. Choctaw Coal and Railway Company.

———— ∞∞ ————

Q. During the Civil War, who served as the commander of Confederate forces in Indian Territory?

A. General Sam Bell Maxey.

———— ∞∞ ————

Q. In 1911, what resident of Ardmore became the state's second governor?

A. Lee Cruce.

Q. Who filed the property deeds in 1891 that led to the establishment of Yukon?

A. A. N. Spencer.

Q. What Native-American peoples comprised the Five Civilized Tribes?

A. Cherokee, Choctaw, Chickasaw, Creek, and Seminole.

Q. Who established the first flour mill in Indian Territory in 1877?

A. J. H. "Jake" Bartles.

Q. What hose and chemical truck served as Oklahoma City's first motorized fire apparatus?

A. 1910 America LaFrance.

Q. In 1820, where was the first court established within the borders of present-day Oklahoma?

A. Miller.

Q. Between 1870 and 1872, what railroad line secured the first north-south tracks to cross the Territory?

A. Missouri, Kansas, and Texas (KATY).

Q. What federal legislation separated the Panhandle area from Texas?

A. The Compromise of 1850.

Q. Opened during Indian Territory days, what Spiro establishment is one of Oklahoma's oldest retailers?

A. Redwine's Hardware.

Q. Following the Civil War, what Native Americans were forced to relinquish much of their vast land holdings to other tribes, due to alliance with the Confederate States of America?

A. Cherokee.

Q. Since 1911, what military facility has been the home of the U.S. Army Field Artillery Center and School?

A. Fort Sill.

Q. From what town did federal troops deport some 200 coal miners and their families to Arkansas in an 1894 labor dispute?

A. Alderson.

Q. What was the name of the "Boomer" tent settlement on the Chikaskia River during the summer of 1884, before removed by federal troops?

A. Rock Falls.

Q. In 1826, between what two points was the first road established in Oklahoma?

A. Fort Smith, Arkansas, and Fort Gibson.

Q. From 1856 until statehood, what town served as the capital of the Chickasaw Nation?

A. Tishomingo.

Q. What Guthrie resident was the first woman to be elected to public office in Oklahoma?

A. Cora V. Diehl.

Q. Oklahoma's first governor, Charles N. Haskell, was a native of what state?

A. Ohio.

Q. What institution of higher learning established by the state legislature in 1919 evolved into Northeastern Oklahoma Junior College?

A. Miami School of Mines.

Q. Who founded Dewey in 1898?

A. J. H. "Jake" Bartles.

Q. In May 1824, troops under the command of Colonel Matthew Arbuckle began construction on what military post to help guard the Red River border between the United States and Mexico?

A. Fort Towson.

Q. To help fight the Ku Klux Klan, 1920s governor Martin E. Trapp backed legislation that made it illegal to wear what type of apparel at public gatherings?

A. Masks.

———∞∞———

Q. On October 1, 1858, troops under whose command attacked and killed 90 members of a group of Comanches on their way to Fort Arbuckle for peace talks?

A. Captain Van Dorn (from Fort Belknap, Texas).

———∞∞———

Q. On October 3, 1910, what complex was founded in Oklahoma as a primary national meat processing and packing facility?

A. Stockyards City in Oklahoma City.

———∞∞———

Q. Where was noted evangelist Oral Roberts born in 1918?

A. Ada.

———∞∞———

Q. From 1867 to 1884, what trail across Oklahoma Territory served as the major route for the movement of cattle from Texas to railheads in Kansas?

A. Chisholm Trail.

———∞∞———

Q. At what 1858 battle near Rush Springs did troops of the Second Cavalry kill seventy Comanches?

A. Battle of the Washita Village.

Q. What stage route running from St. Louis, Missouri, to San Francisco, California, opened across Oklahoma in 1858?

A. Butterfield Stage Line.

Q. For what Union casualty of the Civil War battle of Antietam was Fort Reno named?

A. General Jesse L. Reno.

Q. Where is Pretty Boy Floyd buried?

A. Sallisaw.

Q. What Hennessey resident, killed during the Spanish American War at San Juan Hill serving with the Rough Riders, is said to be the first Oklahoman to die on foreign soil in defense of the nation?

A. Roy Cashion.

Q. On July 12, 1839, what town was chosen as the permanent capital of the Cherokee Nation?

A. Tahlequah.

Q. Guthrie resident General J. C. Jamieson fought in Nicaragua under the command of what charismatic leader known as the "grey-eyed man of destiny"?

A. William Walker.

Q. In 1871, what three Kiowa warrior chiefs were incarcerated at Fort Sill following the Jacksonboro wagon train massacre in Texas?

A. Satanta, Satank, and Big Tree.

Q. Still standing and used as retail space, where was the first public school building constructed in the Oklahoma Territory?

A. Edmond (2nd & Boulevard).

Q. Who was Lawton's first attorney?

A. Jake L. Hamon.

Q. Troops of the 7th, 10th, and 19th cavalries bivouacked in what type of structures while constructing Fort Sill?

A. Branch-covered dugouts.

Q. Prior to opening his store and mill on Caney River, where did J. H. "Jake" Bartles run a successful mercantile?

A. Silver Lake (site of the Osage Agency).

Q. In 1866, what town was established as the capital of the Seminole Nation?

A. Wewoka.

Q. What was the first mansion to be built in Oklahoma City?

A. Overholser Mansion (built by Henry Overholser).

Q. During its oilboom in 1926, what town's six-month freight volume on the Rock Island Railroad was second only to the railway volume for Chicago?

A. Seminole.

Q. In what type of facility in Norman did the University of Oklahoma open it first classes in September 1892?

A. A rented store.

Q. What famous Seminole warrior chief is buried at the Fort Gibson National Cemetery?

A. Captain Billy Bowlegs.

Q. In the 1891 land run, who staked the land where Shawnee developed?

A. Etta Ray.

Q. What two-term principal chief of the Choctaw suggested in 1866 that the proposed territory comprised of Indian lands be called "Oklahoma"?

A. Allen Wright.

Q. When first chartered on October 11, 1906, by what name was Phillips University known?

A. Oklahoma Christian University.

Q. What Native American, who has been called "Oklahoma's Pocahontas," was the first woman to be awarded a Congressional Medal?

A. Milly Francis.

———— ∞∞ ————

Q. In 1835, what type of federal jurisdiction in Arkansas was extended to cover the lands in Indian Territory?

A. Criminal jurisdiction.

———— ∞∞ ————

Q. In 1891, an Arapaho named Sitting Bull almost led the tribes at Fort Sill into open rebellion by promoting what messianic Indian movement sweeping the West?

A. The Ghost Dance (or Messiah Craze).

———— ∞∞ ————

Q. According to the first government town site survey, what was the official population of Tulsa in 1900?

A. 1,390.

———— ∞∞ ————

Q. What fort was operational on the Arkansas River near present-day Spiro from 1834 to 1838?

A. Fort Coffee.

———— ∞∞ ————

Q. In July 1892, what band of desperados robbed a train of $17,000 at the Adair depot?

A. The Dalton Gang.

Q. What secretary of war during the Hoover administration graduated from Bacone University in 1905?

A. Patrick J. Hurley.

———∞∞∞———

Q. A 1825 treaty with what tribe fixed the eastern border of present-day Oklahoma from Fort Smith, Arkansas, south to the Red River?

A. Choctaw.

———∞∞∞———

Q. What 1880 presidential candidate on the Greenback ticket later became a resident of Guthrie?

A. General J. B. Weaver.

———∞∞∞———

Q. In 1910, when the first bridge was constructed across the South Canadian River at Purcell, what was the exorbitant toll to cross the structure?

A. $10.

———∞∞∞———

Q. Who was elected as Drumright's chief of police in 1916 to clean out the outlaw element in the rough-and-tough boom-town?

A. "Fighting Jack" Ary.

———∞∞∞———

Q. The infamous Dalton Boys' parents were homesteaders near what Kingfisher County community?

A. Dover.

Q. Near what town did the last Comanche chief, Quanah Parker, and his five wives settle in 1890?

A. Cache.

———⊗⊗⊗———

Q. In 1852, what became the first town officially "incorporated" in Oklahoma under Cherokee law?

A. Tahlequah.

———⊗⊗⊗———

Q. In 1905, leaders of the Five Civilized Tribes convened and drew up a constitution for what proposed Indian state?

A. Sequoyah.

———⊗⊗⊗———

Q. Prior to World War II, where was the first officially designated seaplane base in Oklahoma?

A. Lake Overholser, Oklahoma City.

———⊗⊗⊗———

Q. In the winter of 1868, troops under the command of what general attacked the camp of Chief Black Kettle on the Washita near present-day Cheyenne, and killed or wounded some two hundred men, women, and children?

A. General George A. Custer.

———⊗⊗⊗———

Q. Where did aviator Wiley Post and Will Rogers die in a 1935 plane crash?

A. Point Barrow, Alaska.

Q. In 1904, what independent, United Methodist–related college was founded in Oklahoma?

A. Oklahoma City University.

───∞∞∞───

Q. During the Truman administration, what Pawhuska banker and rancher served as assistant treasurer of the United States?

A. Maybelle Kennedy (1952–53).

───∞∞∞───

Q. What federal legislation of 1906 allowed delegates to convene in Guthrie and draw up a constitution for the proposed state of Oklahoma?

A. Enabling Act.

───∞∞∞───

Q. In June 1921, a major race riot left 36 persons dead and what African-American business and residential area of Tulsa in ashes?

A. Greenwood district.

───∞∞∞───

Q. What passionate protester against the occupation of Creek Nation land by white settlers led the Crazy Snake Rebellion?

A. Chitto Harjo.

───∞∞∞───

Q. In 1985, who became the first woman to serve as principal chief of the Cherokee Nation?

A. Wilma Mankiller.

Q. Who established the now-vanished Fort Nichols on the banks of Carrizzo Creek in 1865, about four miles east of the present Oklahoma–New Mexico border?

A. Kit Carson.

Q. The opening day of the Kiowa-Apache-Comanche reservation by lottery to white settlers in July 1901 drove the population of El Reno to what figure?

A. Approximately 145,000.

Q. In 1862, what tribe, camping near Fort Cobb and suspected of cannibalism, was virtually exterminated by Osage, Shawnee, Delaware, and Caddo warriors?

A. Tonkawa.

Q. Between resigning as governor of Tennessee and becoming president of the Republic of Texas, what colorful politician lived in the vicinity of present-day Gore?

A. Sam Houston.

Q. What notorious female outlaw lived on a farm along the Canadian River near Eufaula?

A. Belle Starr.

ARTS & LITERATURE

C H A P T E R   F O U R

Q. What newspaper was founded at Fort Gibson in 1888?

A. *Indian Arrow.*

———∞∞∞———

Q. What Fairfax-born dancer is generally regarded as the United States' first great prima ballerina?

A. Maria Tallchief.

———∞∞∞———

Q. What Oklahoman composed the classic folk song "This Land Is Your Land"?

A. Woody Guthrie.

———∞∞∞———

Q. Where was cartoonist Chester Gould, who created *Dick Tracy,* born?

A. Pawnee.

———∞∞∞———

Q. What Oklahoma playwright created *Knives from Syria, A Lantern to See By,* and *Green Grow the Lilacs*?

A. Lynn Riggs.

Q. Who painted the murals depicting the history of northwest Oklahoma at the entrance of Woodard's Plains Indians and Pioneers Museum?

A. Paul Laune.

─────※─────

Q. What is the award-winning quarterly journal published by the National Cowboy Hall of Fame in Oklahoma City?

A. *Persimmon Hill.*

─────※─────

Q. Who created the centennial monument in Ponca City's Centennial Plaza?

A. Jo Saylors.

─────※─────

Q. What book championing the conservation of natural resources was published by Senator Robert S. Kerr in 1960?

A. *Land, Wood, and Water.*

─────※─────

Q. Where did anti-booze crusader Carry A. Nation publish her prohibitionist newspaper, *The Hatchet,* in 1905?

A. Guthrie.

─────※─────

Q. What noted illustrator and painter of the early frontier visited the Wichita Mountains during the 1834 Leavenworth-Dodge expedition?

A. George Catlin.

Q. With Merle Haggard, what native of Oklahoma co-wrote the country classic "Today I Started Loving You Again"?

A. Bonnie Owens.

———⊗⊗⊗———

Q. What Choctaw County town was named in honor of the French author of *The Hunchback of Notre Dame* and *Les Misérables*?

A. Hugo (for Victor Marie Hugo).

———⊗⊗⊗———

Q. What Shawnee physician composed "Home On The Range"?

A. Dr. Brewster Higlers.

———⊗⊗⊗———

Q. What Osage leader bequeathed his extensive collection of tribal costumes, crafts, and memorabilia to the Smithsonian Institution in Washington, D. C.?

A. Chief Bacon Rind.

———⊗⊗⊗———

Q. In 1984, what dance company was created in Cleveland County to provide performance opportunities to young dancers?

A. Norman Ballet Company.

———⊗⊗⊗———

Q. What 1955 Bartlesville office building was design by famed architect Frank Lloyd Wright?

A. Price Tower.

Q. Where was the first library established in the Oklahoma Territory?

A. Edmond.

———∞∞∞———

Q. What 1930s play by Oklahoma dramatist Mary McDougal Axelson was adapted to film and shown internationally?

A. *Life Begins.*

———∞∞∞———

Q. In 1916, what African-American newspaper was established in Oklahoma City?

A. *Black Dispatch.*

———∞∞∞———

Q. What monthly publication is produced by the Oklahoma Romance Writers of America?

A. *The OK Corral.*

———∞∞∞———

Q. What Duncan-born composer penned the Kingston Trio's "Greenback Dollar," Steppenwolf's "The Pusher," Three Dog Night's "Joy to the World," and Ringo Starr's "No No Song"?

A. Hoyt Axton.

———∞∞∞———

Q. Who donated their mansion to become the home of Tulsa's Philbrook Museum of Art?

A. Waite and Genevieve Phillips.

Q. The Picture in Scripture Amphitheater in Disney is the home to what outdoor theatrical production?

A. *The Man Who Ran.*

———— ∞∞ ————

Q. What periodical for the Cheyenne and Arapaho Agency was published at Darlington from 1879 to 1886?

A. *Cheyenne Transporter.*

———— ∞∞ ————

Q. Who was the first conductor of the Tulsa Philharmonic?

A. H. Arthur Brown.

———— ∞∞ ————

Q. Okmulgee is the hometown of what producer of public radio documentaries, primarily on the subject of Native Americans?

A. Peggy Berryhill.

———— ∞∞ ————

Q. The mural in the state capitol of a World War I soldier preparing to meet his troops was painted by what artist in Paris in 1921?

A. Gilbert White.

———— ∞∞ ————

Q. What is the state song?

A. "Oklahoma."

———— ∞∞ ————

Q. Known for his use of Native-American themes in various media, where was artist Austin Real Rider born in 1941?

A. Pawnee.

Q. In 1989, Robert Annesley was awarded what title by the Five Civilized Tribes Museum?

A. Master Artist.

———❀———

Q. Who created the 1890 *Illustrated History of Oklahoma*?

A. Marion Tuttle Rook.

———❀———

Q. What eminent architect designed the Bartlesville-area home Shin 'en Kan (House of the Far Away Heart)?

A. Bruce Goff.

———❀———

Q. In 1941, the United States Department of the Interior selected what Oklahoma Kiowa Indian artist to create murals for its Washington, D.C., facilities?

A. Stephen Mopope.

———❀———

Q. What newspaper was established just prior to the Land Run of 1893 to promote the creation of the new town of Blackwell Rock?

A. *Blackwell Eagle.*

———❀———

Q. Where is the office and museum of the World Organization of China Painters?

A. Oklahoma City.

Q. What slave on a Choctaw plantation close to Doaksville is credited with having originated such classic spirituals as "Swing Low, Sweet Chariot," "Steal Away to Jesus," and "I'm A Rollin'" in the 1840s?

A. "Uncle" Wallace Willis.

———

Q. What town is known as the "City of Murals"?

A. Hominy.

———

Q. Who created the statue of Will Rogers that stands in the foyer of the Will Rogers Memorial in Claremore?

A. Jo Davidson.

———

Q. What historical writer authored the 1934 *Rise and Fall of the Choctaw Republic*?

A. Angie Debo,

———

Q. In 1932, 22 paintings by what Oklahoman became a part of the San Francisco Museum of Art's permanent collection?

A. Woodrow "Woody" Crumbo.

———

Q. Where was the first children's primer in the Creek language published in 1835?

A. Union.

Q. What stately house is home to the Ponca City Art Center?

A. Soldani Mansion.

Q. The Tulsa Ballet Theatre was founded in 1956 by what two internationally known dancers?

A. Moscelyne Larkin and Roman Jasinski.

Q. What favorite fiddler of territorial days composed the popular dance tune "Uncle Paul"?

A. Paul Toupin.

Q. What non-profit corporation was set up in 1976 to develop the arts and artists across the state?

A. Oklahoma Arts Institute.

Q. Oklahoma-raised singer/songwriter Roger Miller composed what Broadway musical?

A. *Big River.*

Q. Noted for his work in tempera, what Hanna-born artist started a career in art in his mid-30s?

A. Albert Harjo.

Q. What world-renown Oklahoma conductor was named "Oklahoma Musician of the Year" for 1992?

A. Joel Levine.

Q. Though an attempt had been made by the *Tahlequah Telephone* in 1889, what 1892 Ardmore newspaper became the first successful daily in the territory?

A. *Daily Chieftain.*

———∞∞∞———

Q. Performed in the Wichita Mountains near Lawton, what is the title of the longest running outdoor passion play in America?

A. *The Prince of Peace.*

———∞∞∞———

Q. Where does the Lachen Meyer Creative Arts Center provide opportunities for local artists and students?

A. Cushing.

———∞∞∞———

Q. What choral group from Oklahoma City performed in 1939 at the New York World's Fair?

A. Oklahoma Symphonic Choir.

———∞∞∞———

Q. What Creek newspaper was first published in 1876 at Muskogee?

A. *Indian Journal.*

———∞∞∞———

Q. Oreland C. Joe created the 22-foot bronze statue of what Ponca chief, which pays tribute to the six Native-American tribes around Ponca City?

A. Chief Standing Bear.

Q. What is the only orchestra in the state that maintains a full-time core of professional staff musicians?

A. Tulsa Philharmonic.

Q. The colorful and accurate story of old Fort Sill is covered in what book by Captain W. S. Nye?

A. *Carbine and Lance.*

Q. What Chickasaw mezzo-soprano, who performed with the Chicago Civic Opera in the 1930s and 1940s, was born near Ardmore?

A. Lushanya (Tessie Mobley).

Q. From its inception in the early 1960s, what Oklahoma City musical theatre has become known as the "Central Oklahoma Broadway Connection"?

A. Lyric Theatre.

Q. What much-published Oklahoma poet of the first half of the twentieth century penned and illustrated such collections as *Paradise Lost, Leaves from a Grass Home,* and *Memory Rooms?*

A. Don Blanding.

Q. What organization sponsors the annual Winter Tales Storytelling Festival?

A. The Art Council of Oklahoma City.

Q. In 1843–44, what much-traveled artist painted portraits and snapped daguerreotypes of intertribal council members at Tahlequah and Webber Falls, and Army officers at Fort Gibson?

A. John Mix Stanley.

———∞———

Q. What Oklahoma City architect designed Guthrie's huge Scottish Rite Temple?

A. J. C. Parr.

———∞———

Q. Who founded the "Holy City" complex and pageant facility in the Wichita Mountains?

A. Reverend Anthony Mark Wallock.

———∞———

Q. What artist born in Norman in 1943 is noted for his masterful silverpoint and goldpoint drawings?

A. Robert Annesley.

———∞———

Q. What premier 150-voice choral ensemble's performances are accompanied by the Oklahoma City Philharmonic Orchestra?

A. Canterbury Choral Society.

———∞———

Q. On June 19, 1886, what became the first newspaper in the Panhandle?

A. *Beaver City Pioneer.*

Q. What Claremore-born sculptor is known for the monuments *The Cherokee Kid, The Spirit of Naval Aviation, The Free and the Brave,* and *All I Know is What I Read in the Papers*?

A. Sandra Van Zandt.

———⚬∞∞⚬———

Q. What classic novel about the Oklahoma Territory was penned by Edna Ferber?

A. *Cimarron.*

———⚬∞∞⚬———

Q. On December 4, 1948, what was the first opera presented by the newly formed Tulsa Opera Club?

A. *La Traviata.*

———⚬∞∞⚬———

Q. What 1940 book by Angie Debo dealt with the defrauding of the Indians of Oklahoma?

A. *And Still the Waters Run.*

———⚬∞∞⚬———

Q. What 1929 novel by George Washington Ogden gave a vivid and colorful picture of Perry's early days?

A. *Sooner Land.*

———⚬∞∞⚬———

Q. Roy Harris, who composed *Time Suite,* was born near what town?

A. Chandler.

Q. What Oklahoma native authored *Political Woman* and *The New Presidential Elite*?

A. Jeane Jordan Kirkpatrick.

Q. In 1882, what western illustrator, painter, and sculptor came down the Chisholm Trail to gather information at Fort Reno and the Darlington Indian Agency for later works?

A. Frederic Remington.

Q. What artist was named "Outstanding Oklahoman of the Year" in 1976, and "Outstanding Indian of the Year" in 1979?

A. Fred Beaver.

Q. *Oklahoma Town* and *No More Trumpets* are collections of short stories created for national magazines of the 1930s and 1940s by what Oklahoma writer?

A. George Milburn.

Q. What gospel music composer, best known for "I'll Fly Away," was born near Spiro in 1905?

A. Albert E. Brumley.

Q. What town's professional theater company presents Shakespeare in the Park, mid-May through August?

A. Edmond, at Hafer Park.

Q. What artist, who graduated from Oklahoma State University in 1974, received the 1987 Red Earth Grand Award for his work?

A. Benjamin Harjo, Jr.

Q. What September celebration in Weatherford features crafts, performing arts, and concerts?

A. Southwest Festival of Arts.

Q. For what sculptor was Vinita named?

A. Vinnie Ream.

Q. What Metropolitan Opera tenor spent his childhood in Sayre?

A. Giuseppi Bentonelli (Joseph Benton).

Q. In the epic John Steinbeck novel *The Grapes of Wrath*, the Joad family started their California trek from what eastern Oklahoma town?

A. Sallisaw.

Q. What Cherokee writer authored the best-selling novel *Brothers Three*?

A. John Milton Oskison.

Q. In 1888, where were the early issues of the *Oklahoma City Times* newspaper printed?

A. Wichita, Kansas.

Q. What prolific Oklahoma City composer of the first half of the twentieth century was known for his teaching pieces for piano?

A. Edwin Vaile McIntyre.

Q. The unique problems of farm women in the Cherokee Strip is the basis for what Dora Aydelotte novel?

A. *Trumpets Calling.*

Q. Where was historical illustrator and painter Clyde Heron born in 1929?

A. Ardmore.

Q. What writer, known for her 1940s syndicated column "A Woman's Viewpoint," published the *Cherokee Republic* in Cherokee?

A. Lucia Loomis (Mrs. Walter Ferguson).

Q. Where is the annual Nescatunga Arts Festival held?

A. Alva.

Q. Shawnee's first newspaper, the *Shawnee Chief*, was renamed and moved to what adjoining town?

A. Tecumseh.

Q. Although built on an orchestral heritage dating back to the 1920s, what was the first season for the Oklahoma Philharmonic orchestra?

A. 1988–89.

―――――

Q. Each summer, where is the Oklahoma Shakespearean Festival held?

A. Southeastern Oklahoma State University, Durant.

―――――

Q. In what year did the Tulsa Philharmonic Society come into existence?

A. 1948.

―――――

Q. Who served as chair of the School of Art at the University of Tulsa from 1945 to 1963?

A. Alexandre Hogue.

―――――

Q. Featuring art exhibits along with performing arts and musical presentations, what Beckham County town hosts the annual Fall Festival of the Arts?

A. Elk City.

―――――

Q. Founded in 1896, what was Muskogee's first daily newspaper?

A. *Morning Times.*

Q. What native Oklahoman created the large historical murals that hang in the rotunda of the state capitol?

A. Charles Banks.

Q. Who penned the novel *Rider of the Cherokee Strip*?

A. Evan G. Barnard.

Q. Where is the state art collection on permanent display?

A. Kirkpatrick Center, Oklahoma City.

Q. What unique sculpture competition is held in Tulsa each July?

A. Arkansas River Sand Castle Contest.

Q. What composer from Seminole created numerous teaching pieces for piano, voice, and violin in the 1930s and 1940s?

A. Charles B. Macklin.

Q. What University of Tulsa graduate created the cartoon strip *Broom Hilda*?

A. Russell Myers.

Q. Where is the Southern Plains Indian Museum, featuring exhibits of Native-American artists and craftsmen?

A. Anadarko.

Q. What Oklahoma sculptor created such notable works as *Offering to the Great Spirit* and *As Long As the Waters Flow*?

A. Allan Houser.

——— ∞∞∞ ———

Q. Checotah was home to what 1954 Pulitzer Prize winner?

A. Jim G. Lucas.

——— ∞∞∞ ———

Q. Bess Gowans, Ralph and Ione Sassano, Mary Helen Markham, and Beverly Bliss established what organization in 1948 to promote opera in Tulsa?

A. Tulsa Opera Club.

——— ∞∞∞ ———

Q. What Watonga newspaper man and territorial governor wrote the popular 1892 novel *The Jayhawks: A Tale of the Border War*?

A. Thompson B. Ferguson.

——— ∞∞∞ ———

Q. In 1990, who became the first Native American to present a solo Indian flute concert at New York's Carnegie Hall?

A. Doc (Joyce Lee Tate) Nevaquaya.

——— ∞∞∞ ———

Q. Where is the Firehouse Art Center, which features regional art and crafts?

A. Norman.

Q. What painter, best known for his depictions of the Seminole people, was educated at Muskogee's Bacone College?

A. Fred Beaver.

Q. Founded in 1983, what non-profit organization focuses on musical theater, specifically on the presentation of the works of U. S. Gilbert and Sir Arthur Sullivan?

A. The Gilbert & Sullivan Society of Tulsa.

Q. What nationally famous pottery works was founded in Sapulpa in 1933?

A. Frankoma Pottery.

Q. Where is the State Capital Publishing Museum, which features vintage printing equipment and newspaper memorabilia?

A. Guthrie.

Q. What sculptor and stone carver, born at Concho, is best known for *The Blue Corn People*?

A. Charles Pratt.

Q. What is the official state musical instrument?

A. Fiddle.

Q. In 1896–97, what artist painted some 125 portraits of notable Kiowas and Comanche Indians, including Geronimo?

A. Elbridge Ayer Burbank.

Q. What annual summer event at Bartlesville features the works of Wolfgang Amadeus Mozart?

A. OK Mozart Festival.

Q. What self-taught Indian artist from El Reno, in addition to his painting and bronze works, is one of the nation's foremost forensic artists?

A. Harvey Pratt.

Q. At what amphitheatre in the Cherokee Heritage Center, just south of Tahlequah, is the bittersweet story of the Cherokee people told?

A. Tsa-La-Gi Theatre.

Q. What native Oklahoman wrote the historical books *Death on the Prairie* and *Death in the Desert*, which deal with Indians in the West?

A. Paul I. Wellman.

Q. Where in Edmond is the Edmond Blues & Jazz Festival and the Edmond Art Association Show held each May?

A. Hafer Park.

Q. What Tulsa facility is home to the world's largest and most comprehensive collection of American western art?

A. Gilcrease Museum.

Q. Where was the short-lived *Chickasaw and Choctaw Herald* newspaper published in 1858 and 1859?

A. Tishomingo.

Q. What early nineteenth-century American writer made note in his book *A Tour On The Prairies* of his overnight camp at a place called Bear's Glen, near the juncture of the Cimarron and Arkansas Rivers?

A. Washington Irving.

Q. Where may one visit the International Photograph Hall of Fame and Museum?

A. Omniplex, Oklahoma City.

Q. What participant in the 1893 Cherokee Outlet Run later captured the event on canvas in his work *The Run*?

A. John Noble.

Q. Oklahoma Festival Ballet and Modern Repertory Dance Theatre are resident dance companies of what university?

A. University of Oklahoma.

Q. What Oklahoma biographer of the 1930s and 1940s penned works on Kit Carson and Sitting Bull?

A. Stanley Vestal (W. S. Campbell).

———

Q. Where is the Joe Stribling Arts and Crafts Show held each year on the Saturday before Mother's Day?

A. Davenport.

———

Q. What sculptor, painter, and founding member of Cowboy Artists of America was raised in Oklahoma?

A. Joe Beeler.

———

Q. On what campus is the Fred Jones, Jr., Museum of Art?

A. University of Oklahoma, Norman.

———

Q. What quarterly publication is issued by the Oklahoma Historical Society?

A. *The Chronicles of Oklahoma.*

———

Q. During the first half of the twentieth century, who was the most prolific writer of books pertaining to the Five Civilized Tribes?

A. Betty Blake Rogers.

———

Q. What downtown Oklahoma City theatrical attraction focuses on works by contemporary playwrights?

A. Carpenter Square Theatre.

Q. The old pop tune "Especially For You" was written by what Oklahoma City composer?

A. Phil Grogan.

───── ∞∞ ─────

Q. What Carnegie-born artist created murals for the RCA Building in New York?

A. Woody Big Bow.

───── ∞∞ ─────

Q. Dating back to the early 1900s, what is the longest running university performing arts series in the state?

A. Allied Arts, Oklahoma State University.

───── ∞∞ ─────

Q. In 1916, what organization was created to promote art in Oklahoma?

A. Association of Oklahoma Artists.

───── ∞∞ ─────

Q. Featuring some of the nation's most notable four-string banjo strummers, where is the Jazz Banjo Festival held?

A. Guthrie.

───── ∞∞ ─────

Q. Noted for his free-flowing and poetic works in acrylic, tempera, and gouache, where was Ponca painter Mars Biggoose born?

A. Pawnee.

Q. Who authored a book about Oklahoma's runestones entitled *In Plain Sight: Old World Records in Ancient America*?

A. Gloria Farley.

Q. Who wrote the Will Rogers book *The Cherokee Kid*?

A. David N. Milsten.

Q. Founded in Muskogee on March 19, 1888, what was the first organization to represent the newspapers of the territory?

A. Indian Territory Press Association.

Q. Who was the founding director of the Art Department at Bacone College?

A. Acee Blue Eagle.

Q. In 1936, what Oklahoman received a Pulitzer Prize for his editorial writing?

A. George B. "Deak" Parker.

Q. Where is the Samuel H. Kress collection of Italian Renaissance and Baroque art housed?

A. Philbrook Museum of Art, Tulsa.

Q. Who authored the 1941 history of the Creek Nation, *The Road to Disappearance*?

A. Angie Debo.

Q. What newspaper started at Vinita in 1882?

A. *Indian Chieftain.*

Q. Founded in the late 1970s, what organization is recognized as Oklahoma's first modern dance company?

A. Prairie Dance Theatre, Oklahoma City.

Q. What magazine, giving insight into the history, activities, and culture of Oklahoma, was established in 1956 by the Oklahoma Department of Tourism?

A. *Oklahoma Today.*

Q. Who created the two life-sized public bronze sculpture pieces on display in Altus, *Crossing the Red* and *The Vision Seeker*?

A. H. Holden.

Q. What biographical work by Osage writer John Joseph Mathews detailed the life of Indian agent, Major Laban J. Miles?

A. *Wah'Kon-Tah.*

Q. Who painted murals for the officers' mess on the battleship USS *Oklahoma*?

A. Blue Eagle.

Q. Where is the Canterbury Arts Festival held?

A. Edmond.

Q. The works of what noted frontier photographer and Blackwell area homesteader are on permanent display at Blackwell's Top of Oklahoma Museum?

A. W. S. Prettyman.

Q. Where was Acee Blue Eagle born in 1909?

A. Wichita Reservation near Anadarko.

Q. What Edward Donahoe 1930s novel dealt with the social and financial leeches in an oil boomtown?

A. *Madness in the Heart.*

Q. Who became an artist-director with the Tulsa Ballet Theatre in 1995?

A. Marcello Angelini.

Q. What is the state's only independent newspaper that serves all of Oklahoma's federally recognized Indian Nations?

A. *Oklahoma Indian Times.*

Q. Where is the Quilt Museum?

A. Oklahoma City.

Q. What first director of the University of Oklahoma's School of Art promoted and mentored the famous "Kiowa Five" Native-American artists?

A. Oscar B. Jacobson.

Q. Who composed the popular western tune "Oklahoma Hills"?

A. Jack and Woody Guthrie.

Q. Allan Houser, considered the "patriarch of Native-American sculptors," was born where in 1914?

A. Fort Sill.

Q. What facility, built on the campus of Bacone College in 1932, houses one of the finest privately owned collections of traditional and contemporary Native-American art in the nation?

A. Ataloa Lodge.

Q. In whose barn was the Muskogee's first opera house opened in 1879?

A. Joshua Ross.

Q. What descendent of Kiowa warrior chief Satanta, who is known for his sculpture, was co-creator of murals at the Kiowa Tribal Complex?

A. Sherman Chaddlesone.

Q. What non-profit organization in southwestern Oklahoma dedicates its energies to the presentation of ballet?

A. Lawton City Ballet.

Q. Recipient of the Governor's Arts Award, what is Oklahoma City's oldest community theater?

A. Jewel Box Theatre.

Q. What mural in the state capitol by Chickasaw artist Mike Larsen commemorates five world-famous Oklahoma Indian ballerinas?

A. *Flight of Spirit.*

Q. Who created the musical *Oklahoma!*?

A. Richard Rogers and Oscar Hammerstein II.

Q. In 1889, what newspaper, owned and edited by James S. Standley, superseded the *Atoka Independent*?

A. *The Indian Citizen.*

Q. What town is home to the Red Carpet Community Theatre?

A. Elk City.

Q. What Native-American painter and silversmith was born near Lexington in 1912?

A. Woodrow "Woody" Crumbo.

SPORTS & LEISURE

CHAPTER FIVE

Q. In the 1912 Olympic Games, what Oklahoman became the first athlete to win both the decathlon and pentathlon?

A. Jim Thorpe.

Q. Known for its Pecan Festival, what town holds the world record for largest pecan pie, largest pecan cookie, and largest pecan brownie?

A. Okmulgee.

Q. Where were Paul and Lloyd Warner, star players for the Pittsburgh Pirates, born?

A. Harrah.

Q. What Talihina summer event is built around bovine waste?

A. Cow Patty Caper.

Q. Sallisaw is home to what thoroughbred racetrack?

A. Blue Ribbon Downs.

Q. Who was the head baseball coach at the University of Oklahoma from 1942 to 1967?

A. Jack Baer.

Q. What are the team colors at the University of Central Oklahoma in Edmond?

A. Bronze and blue.

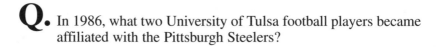

Q. In 1986, what two University of Tulsa football players became affiliated with the Pittsburgh Steelers?

A. Mike Williams and Gordon Brown.

Q. Where is the first bubble-topped custom car created in 1960 by Starbird?

A. National Rod & Custom Car Hall of Fame (Afton).

Q. What was the hometown of New York Giants pitcher Carl Hubbell?

A. Meeker.

Q. What major Blaine County lake is the site of an annual Walleye Rodeo?

A. Canton.

Q. Featuring thousands of Harley-Davidson motorcycles, where is the annual Oklahoma State H.O.G. Rally held each fall?

A. Eufaula.

Q. What offensive tackle at the University of Tulsa was a first-round draft pick of the Seattle Seahawks, and later played for the Steelers and the Jets?

A. Steve August.

Q. Where is the Western Okie Spokie Bike Ride held each July?

A. Elk City.

Q. What defensive end from the University of Oklahoma played with the Chicago Bears in 1991 and 1992, and then with the New Orleans Saints in 1993 and 1994?

A. Tom Backes.

Q. What Oklahoman received the title of "The World's Greatest Dribbler"?

A. Marques Haynes.

Q. At age 20, what former Foyil High School track star claimed the $25,000 prize, and saved the family farm, in the 1928 Route 66 promotional 3,400-mile-long "Bunion Derby" footrace?

A. Andy Payne.

Q. What 1959 All-Big-Eight football player was the first black student-athlete at the University of Oklahoma?

A. Prentice Gautt.

———&&&———

Q. What are the team colors of Oklahoma Baptist University's Bison and Lady Bison?

A. Green and gold.

———&&&———

Q. In October 1997, University of Tulsa's volleyball team set two school records with how many kills and assists in a single match against the Missouri–Kansas City Kangaroos?

A. 83 kills, and 71 assists.

———&&&———

Q. What offensive tackle from the University of Oklahoma who played on OU's 1974 and 1975 National Championship teams later played for the Detroit Lions and Baltimore-Indianapolis Colts?

A. Karl Baldischwiler.

———&&&———

Q. Following a 1961 tryout, what Crescent-born basketball player spent the next 24 years with the Harlem Globetrotters?

A. Hubert "Geese" Ausbie.

———&&&———

Q. What University of Oklahoma defensive tackle was drafted by the Dallas Cowboys in 1978, and moved to the Oakland Raiders in 1980?

A. David Hudgens.

Q. What town annually builds a one-day event around the preparation and devouring of the world's largest onion burger?

A. El Reno.

———∞∞∞———

Q. Where is the Grand National Quail Hunt held in early December?

A. Enid.

———∞∞∞———

Q. What baseball player from Oklahoma is credited with having made golf's longest hole-in-one at 427 yards in 1961?

A. Lou Kretlow.

———∞∞∞———

Q. In 1943 and 1946, what Oklahoma State University (A&M) football player led the nation in pass receptions?

A. Neill Armstrong.

———∞∞∞———

Q. Where is the state's largest amateur western show held each July?

A. Pawhuska.

———∞∞∞———

Q. In 1967, 1968, and 1972, what Oklahoman was the PRCA World Champion Steerwrestler?

A. Roy Duvall.

———∞∞∞———

Q. Where is the Champion Cornstalk bow-and-arrow shoot held each Labor Day?

A. Tahlequah.

Q. Because of his quickness and movements on the mound, what nickname was given the 1940s and 1950s Oklahoma-born pitcher Harry Brecheen?

A. "The Cat."

Q. What native of Hominy established the much-coveted Jim Thorpe Award for best college defensive back?

A. Lynne Draper.

Q. What Oklahoma State University football coach led teams to a 1944 Cotton Bowl win and a 1945 Sugar Bowl victory?

A. Jim Lookabaugh.

Q. What is the name of Oklahoma City's outdoor water park?

A. White Water Bay.

Q. During his 20 years in the major leagues, Oklahoma native Lindy McDaniel pitched in how many innings?

A. 2,140.

Q. In 1985, what University of Tulsa golf coach was selected as National Coach of the Year?

A. Dale McNamara.

Q. Southwestern Oklahoma State University's Bulldogs and Lady Bulldogs wear what team colors?

A. Navy and white.

Q. Where is the National Softball Hall of Fame and Stadium?

A. Oklahoma City.

Q. Out of 3,984 times at bat, how many times did Oklahoma native Dale Mitchell strike out?

A. 119.

Q. In the 1980s, what women's basketball star at Southwestern State University was chosen four times as NAIA Player of the Year?

A. Kelli Litsch.

Q. What offensive tackle at Oklahoma State University was a two-time All-Big-Eight player and joined the Chicago Bears in 1986?

A. Paul Blair.

Q. What Oklahoma City college's sports teams are nicknamed the Prophets?

A. Oklahoma Baptist College and Institute.

Q. Who is recognized as the most successful baseball coach in the history of the Big Eight Conference?

A. Gary Ward of OSU.

Q. PGA player Orville Moody is a native of what town?

A. Chickasha.

Q. In 1956, what University of Oklahoma football player was selected as National Lineman of the Year and received the Walter Camp Award?

A. Jerry Tubbs.

Q. What Oklahoma State University rusher, who was the Big Eight Conference's Offensive Player of the Year in 1985 and 1987, was named the NFL's Most Valuable Player in 1991?

A. Thurman Thomas.

Q. What Oklahoman is the only NFL coach to go to three Super Bowl games with three different teams?

A. Buddy Ryan.

Q. John Henry Ward, who earned All-American honors at Oklahoma State University, played for what two NFL teams in the 1970s?

A. Minnesota Vikings and Chicago Bears.

Q. What 11,000-seat arena is the home of Sooner Basketball?

A. Lloyd Noble Center, Norman.

——————

Q. In 1951, University of Oklahoma's Jim Weatherall received what honor as the nation's best interior lineman?

A. Outland Trophy.

——————

Q. Steve Owen, who coached the New York Giants from 1931 to 1953, was born in what town in 1898?

A. Cleo Springs.

——————

Q. In 1990, what University of Tulsa volleyball player set a school individual match record with 35 digs against North Texas?

A. Amy Badalich.

——————

Q. What kicker from Oklahoma State University signed with the New York Jets in 1992 and was a Pro Bowl kicker for the Indianapolis Colts in 1996?

A. Cary Blanchard.

——————

Q. In what two years did pioneer football coach at the University of Oklahoma, Bennie Owen, lead his teams to undefeated seasons?

A. 1911 and 1915.

Q. The Eagles and Lady Eagles are the sports teams of what Oklahoma City college?

A. Oklahoma Christian University.

———∞∞∞———

Q. What Southwestern Oklahoma State University basketball player set a school record of 23 rebounds in a game with Langston University on January 15, 1971?

A. Mort Fraley.

———∞∞∞———

Q. Where is the "biggest open rodeo in the West" held each August?

A. Freedom.

———∞∞∞———

Q. What offensive/defensive halfback, who played at Oklahoma State University from 1955 to 1959, later played one year in the Canadian League, and then with the Dallas Texans and Kansas City Chiefs?

A. Duane Wood.

———∞∞∞———

Q. In 1962, what Oklahoma university received its first-ever national football title when the school won the NAIA National Championship?

A. University of Central Oklahoma.

———∞∞∞———

Q. What early 1920s Missouri Valley national champion wrestler at Oklahoma State University later served as the head wrestling coach at the University of Michigan for some 45 years?

A. Cliff Keen.

Q. What town hosts the Buffalo Mountain Flyers 5-State Regional Hang Glider Competition?

A. Talihina.

———⟨⟩———

Q. In the late 1980s, who became the first football player from the University of Oklahoma to receive the NCAA Top Six Award?

A. Keith Jackson.

———⟨⟩———

Q. What outstanding quarterback at the University of Oklahoma later became a sports commentator in Oklahoma City and worked as a college football analyst for ABC television?

A. Dean Blevins.

———⟨⟩———

Q. Featuring rare and vintage automobiles, where is the Kirk Auto Museum?

A. Ripley,

———⟨⟩———

Q. What University of Oklahoma lineman received All-American honors in 1954 and was drafted by the Chicago Cardinals in 1955?

A. Max Boydston.

———⟨⟩———

Q. Where is the annual 5K Renaissance Run held?

A. Midwest City.

Q. What are the logical team colors of East Central University's Tigers and Lady Tigers?

A. Black and orange.

———⊗⊗⊗———

Q. In 1956, who became Southwestern Oklahoma State University's first basketball player to receive All-American honors?

A. Bill Davis.

———⊗⊗⊗———

Q. What two-time All-American offensive/defensive back for the University of Oklahoma in the mid-1950s went on to play with the Pittsburgh Steelers for eleven years?

A. Clendon Thomas.

———⊗⊗⊗———

Q. In 1989, what former linebacker at the University of Oklahoma became the school's head football coach?

A. Gary Gibbs.

———⊗⊗⊗———

Q. What is the name of Tulsa's AA baseball team?

A. Drillers.

———⊗⊗⊗———

Q. What are the team colors of the Oklahoma City University Chiefs and Lady Chiefs?

A. Columbia blue and white.

Q. The bilking of the citizens of Wetumka of several hundred dollars by a con artist who had promised to bring a circus to town led to what annual festivity?

A. Sucker Day Celebration.

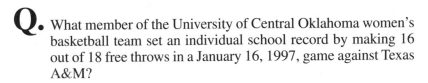

Q. What member of the University of Central Oklahoma women's basketball team set an individual school record by making 16 out of 18 free throws in a January 16, 1997, game against Texas A&M?

A. Christy Heavin.

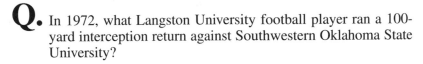

Q. In 1972, what Langston University football player ran a 100-yard interception return against Southwestern Oklahoma State University?

A. Gerald Williams.

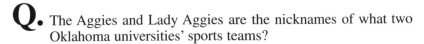

Q. The Aggies and Lady Aggies are the nicknames of what two Oklahoma universities' sports teams?

A. Oklahoma Panhandle State University (crimson and blue), and Cameron University (black and gold).

Q. What Oklahoma State University defensive tackle participated in the 1973 Blue-Gray Game at the Hula Bowl and was drafted the following year by the San Diego Chargers?

A. Bon Boatright.

Q. Where is the Oil & Gas Golf Tournament held?
A. Weatherford.

Q. What was the first bowl game the University of Tulsa played?

A. Sun Bowl (1941).

Q. What baseball pitcher from Oklahoma played with Detroit, Chicago, the St. Louis Browns, Baltimore, and the Kansas City Athletics during the 1940s and 1950s?

A. Lou Kretlow.

Q. What is the name of the "biggest pep rally in Oklahoma," held each September at Oklahoma State University?

A. Orange Peel.

Q. What under-fourteen girls slow pitch softball team was the 1994 USSSA World Champions?

A. Oklahoma Stars.

Q. What early 1950s University of Oklahoma football player became the first person to receive every "lineman of the year" award given at the time?

A. John David "J. D." Roberts.

Q. What team from Moore was the fourteen and under USSSA World Champion for 1998?

A. Moore Magic Girls Slow Pitch Team.

Q. The Eagles and Lady Eagles of Bartlesville Wesleyan College wear what team colors?

A. Red, white, and blue.

Q. In what two years was University of Oklahoma football player Keith Jackson named All-American?

A. 1986 and 1987.

Q. What is the name of Tulsa's minor league hockey team?

A. Oilers.

Q. What Labor Day event at McAlester is billed as the world's largest rodeo held entirely behind prison walls?

A. Oklahoma State Prison Outlaw Rodeo.

Q. What are the team colors of Langston University's Blue Devils?

A. Orange and navy blue.

Q. In 1975, what Oklahoma City team became the ASA Fast Pitch champions?

A. Spirits.

Q. What Ryan-born martial arts expert and actor was named Karate Instructor of the Year in 1975?

A. Chuck Norris.

Q. When was the first pronghorn antelope hunt in the history of the state held?

A. 1966.

Q. What university's sports teams are called the Bronchos?

A. University of Central Oklahoma, Edmond.

Q. Who is the only person to have been named Oklahoma Coach of the Year three times?

A. Elvan George (1951, 1954, and 1957).

Q. Weatherford is the sight of what Suidae-summoning event?

A. World Championship Hog Calling Contest.

Q. What Oklahoman at age 18 went from playing American Legion baseball to playing in the major league with the Dodgers?

A. Calvin Coolidge Julius Caesar Tuskahoma McLish.

Q. Red and white are the team colors of what university?

A. Northwestern Oklahoma State University, Alva.

Q. Following his stay at the University of Oklahoma, where he earned All-American honors in 1971 and 1972, Tom Brahany played for what professional team for nine years?

A. St. Louis Cardinals Football.

Q. What is rated as "Oklahoma's number one light show"?

A. Chickasha's Festival of Lights.

Q. During the 1986 Orange Bowl game, what University of Oklahoma player kicked four field goals against Penn State?

A. Tim Lasher.

Q. What McAlester native served as sports editor of the *Tulsa World* for almost three decades?

A. William Bryan "Bill" Connors, Jr.

Q. In November and May, automobile enthusiasts converge on what town for the Antique Car Swap Meet?

A. Chickasha.

Q. What under-sixteen slow pitch girls softball team was the USSSA World Champions for 1997?

A. Muskogee Saints.

Q. At the 1956 Olympic games in Melbourne, what Oklahoman, along with his three teammates, won a gold medal in the 4x400 relay?

A. J. W. Mashburn.

Q. What expansion team of the short-lived United States Football League played at Tulsa's Skelly Stadium during the 1984 season?

A. Oklahoma Outlaws.

Q. Where is the Oklahoma Steam Threshing and Gas Engine Show held each May?

A. Pawnee.

Q. In the National Championship game against Penn State in 1985 at the Orange Bowl, what University of Oklahoma player was named MVP?

A. Sonny Brown.

Q. What regional fairgrounds complex is at Shawnec?

A. Heart of Oklahoma Exposition Center.

Q. At Super Bowl IX, what Vikings player became the first-ever native Oklahoman to score a touchdown in a Super Bowl game?

A. Terry Brown.

Q. What gaming center in Tucumseh offers state-of-the-art bingo, simulcast horseracing, a Las Vegas Room, and even bowling?

A. Fire Lake Entertainment Center.

Q. Where is the Creek Nation Rodeo and Festival held each August?

A. Okmulgee.

⬥

Q. In what three years did head coach Elvan George lead his East Central State College teams to win the OCC Championship?

A. 1964, 1965, and 1966.

⬥

Q. What softball team for ten and under was the 1996 ASA Slow Pitch Champion?

A. Oklahoma Angels.

⬥

Q. What are the colors of the sports teams at Oral Roberts University in Tulsa?

A. Navy blue, Vegas gold, and white.

⬥

Q. Where is the Panhandle Exposition held each September?

A. Texas County Fairground, in Guymon.

⬥

Q. What defensive end and linebacker at the University of Oklahoma was the school's last two-way player?

A. Steve Zabel.

⬥

Q. Oklahoma-born major league baseball players brothers Paul and Lloyd Waner were respectively known by what nicknames?

A. "Big Poison" and "Little Poison."

Q. What lineman at Phillips University went on to play nine seasons with the Kansas City Cowboys and the New York Giants, before entering a coaching career marked by his "umbrella defense" style?

A. Steve Owen.

Q. Securing the WBA lightweight title in 1981, who is the only world boxing champion from Oklahoma?

A. Sean O'Grady.

Q. What University of Oklahoma running back was named 1972 Player of the Year by the Washington, D. C., Athletic Club?

A. Greg Pruitt.

Q. Although a hunt in limited areas began in 1960, in what year was the first statewide wild turkey hunt held?

A. 1997.

Q. Who drafted University of Oklahoma defensive end Barry Burget in 1980?

A. New England Patriots.

Q. What is the name of Oklahoma City's Central Hockey League team?

A. Blazers.

Q. What University of Oklahoma NCAA wrestling champion won the Big Eight Championship for his class in 1966, 1967, and 1968?

A. Wayne Wells.

Q. Featuring such traditional Native-American activities as horse racing, dancing, and storytelling, where is the annual Comanche Tribal Fair held each October?

A. Lawton.

Q. In 1985, what University of Oklahoma defensive tackle was a Lombardi Award winner and UPI Lineman of the Year?

A. Tony Casillas.

Q. What four-wheeling event is held in the Kiamichi Mountains near Clayton each Memorial Day and Thanksgiving?

A. Jeep Jamboree.

Q. In 1980, who became head coach of the University of Central Oklahoma's women's basketball team and was Lone Star Conference Coach of the Year for 1992?

A. John Keely.

Q. What University of Tulsa volleyball player set a school individual match record for most kills in an October 23, 1997, game against SMU?

A. Kristien Van Lierop.

Q. In what year did Oklahoman Orville Moody win the US Open?

A. 1969.

Q. What wrestler from Del City garnered two Olympic gold medals and six world titles?

A. John Smith.

Q. Before coaching from 1940 to 1962 at El Reno High School, Jenks Simmons played with what two professional football teams?

A. Cleveland Bulldogs and Rhode Island Steamrollers.

Q. What is the hometown of Dallas Cowboys quarterback, Troy Aikman?

A. Henryetta.

Q. Who was Oklahoma State University's last "three-sport" letterman?

A. Dick Soergel.

Q. Where is the world's largest Jackpot Steerwrestling competition held?

A. Checotah.

Q. What guard with the Enid Plainsmen in the late 1940s went on to become one of the all-time winning coaches in the history of college basketball?

A. Don Haskins.

Q. During the 1996 season, what University of Tulsa volleyball player set a school individual season record with 1,103 assists?

A. Mendy March.

Q. What legendary former golf coach at Oklahoma State University designed the course at Weatherford Golf Club?

A. Labion Harris, Sr.

Q. Where was long-time left-handed pitcher for the Saint Louis Cardinals, Harry Brecheen, born?

A. Broken Bow.

Q. What Oklahoma City pari-mutuel facility offers almost year-round racing?

A. Remington Park.

Q. In 1976, what former University of Oklahoma defensive end and linebacker was named the New England Patriots' Most Valuable Player?

A. Steve Zabel.

Q. What town is host to Oklahoma Greyhound Association racing each spring and fall?

A. Altus.

Q. Edmond is the home of what Olympic gymnast and gold medalist?

A. Shannon Miller.

Q. Where was University of Oklahoma defensive back-corner Terry Peters, who later played in both the NFL and in the Canadian League, born?

A. Pauls Valley.

Q. With what professional team did Oklahoma State University running back Kelly Cook sign as a free agent in 1986?

A. Buffalo Bills.

Q. What community is known for its unique "Third of July Celebration"?

A. Dacoma.

Q. Featuring both amateur and Olympic wrestlers, where is the National Wrestling Hall of Fame?

A. Stillwater.

Q. University of Tulsa linebacker Richard Blanchard played with what NFL team in 1972 and 1973, before joining the World Football League's Detroit Wheels in 1974?

A. New England Patriots.

Q. Where is the Hub City Speedway?

A. Clinton.

Q. What nationally recognized polo club in Morman hosts the National Silver Cup and the National President's Cup?

A. Broad Acres Polo Club.

Q. Where in Haskell County is the All Mule Rodeo held each August?

A. Stigler.

Q. What Oklahoman won three NCAA wrestling titles and came in fourth at the 1956 Olympic games?

A. Myron Roderick.

Q. In 1994, what University of Oklahoma baseball coach led his Sooner team to the National Championship and also won National Coach of the Year honors?

A. Larry Cochell.

Q. In 1946, what Oklahoma basketball wizard joined the Harlem Globetrotters?

A. Marques Haynes.

———∞∞∞———

Q. Waynoka hosts what annual hunt on the weekend after Easter?

A. Rattlesnake.

———∞∞∞———

Q. What town is home to the annual Route 66 Challenge, 8K Run, and Two Mile Fun Walk?

A. Davenport.

———∞∞∞———

Q. From 1935 through 1943, how many times did the University of Tulsa football team win or tie as champions of the Missouri Valley Conference?

A. Eight.

———∞∞∞———

Q. What are the names of twin brothers from Ardmore who each served on the coaching staff of an Oklahoma university: one as defensive coordinator at the University of Oklahoma, the other as a defensive coach at Oklahoma State University?

A. Rex Ryan (OU) and Rob Ryan (OSU).

———∞∞∞———

Q. What is the hometown of 16-time world champion bullrider Jim Shoulders?

A. Henryetta.

Q. In play against Phillips University on October 20, 1996, what University of Central Oklahoma women's soccer player set an individual school record by scoring eight points?

A. Stephanie Keiser.

Q. During his career at the University of Oklahoma, what 1975 All-American set a school record 44 tackles for loss?

A. Jimbo Elrod.

Q. What downtown Oklahoma City facility is the home of Redhawks baseball?

A. Bricktown Ballpark.

Q. Which university's sports teams are called the Rangers?

A. Northwestern Oklahoma State University, Alva.

Q. During his stay at the University of Oklahoma, what place kicker set a NCAA record for the most PATS in a row at 125?

A. Uwe von Schamann.

Q. What all-time leading scorer at the University of Tulsa later played for the New England Patriots and the New York Jets?

A. Jason Staurovsky.

Q. Featuring a 10K road race and sand volleyball and baseball tournaments, where is the Sand Plum Sports and Health Festival held each year?

A. Woodward.

———∞∞∞———

Q. What is the "Steerwrestling Capital of the World"?

A. Checotah.

———∞∞∞———

Q. In 1990, what University of Central Oklahoma wrestler became UCO's first four-time national championship winner and the fifth in collegiate history to gain such honors?

A. Johnny Nimmo.

———∞∞∞———

Q. Where is the Oklahoma State Fair held?

A. State Fair Park, Oklahoma City.

———∞∞∞———

Q. At the 1977 Heisman Trophy ceremonies in New York, what University of Oklahoma football player was named the nation's outstanding defensive back?

A. Zac Henderson.

———∞∞∞———

Q. In February 1997, who became the Director of Athletics at the University of Tulsa?

A. Judy MacLeod.

Q. Featuring contests, entertainment, and great food, where is the Kiamichi Owa Chito Festival of the Forest held the third weekend of June?

A. Beavers Bend State Park.

Q. What 1976 All-American offensive guard at Oklahoma State University went on to play for the Green Bay Packers and the San Diego Chargers?

A. Derrel Gofourth.

Q. What Oklahoman pitched 1,137 innings during his big league career with the New York Yankees and the New York Mets?

A. Tom Sturdivant.

Q. Where is the Oklahoma Sports Museum?

A. Guthrie.

Q. What Oklahoma State University quarterback was named MVP at the 1983 Bluebonnet Bowl and five years later earned team MVP with the Detroit Lions?

A. Rusty Hilger.

Q. What April event in Okmulgee features classic cars, hot rods, and customized show cars on display around the downtown square?

A. 50s Bash.

Q. The University of Tulsa joined what athletic conference in July 1996?

A. Western Athletic Conference.

Q. From 1980 to 1985, what former All-Big-Eight defensive end at the University of Oklahoma played in the NFL with the Pittsburgh Steelers?

A. John Goodman.

Q. What city hosted the Red Man All-American Bass Tournament in 1992 and 1994?

A. Muskogee.

Q. What PRCA event is billed as "the toughest rodeo in Oklahoma"?

A. Woodward Elks Rodeo.

Q. What football coach at Ada High School from 1940 to 1958 led his teams to win six state championships in a seven-year period?

A. Elvan George.

Q. In 1974, what girls softball team captured the ASA Fast Pitch Championship for ages fifteen and under?

A. Oklahoma City Racers.

Q. What former University of Tulsa soccer player became the school's head coach for the women's soccer program in 1995?

A. Amy Edwards.

Q. Starting in Denison, Texas, and concluding in Coffeyville, Kansas, what is Oklahoma's only cross-state bicycle race?

A. Oklahoma Freewheel.

Q. What 1946–48 running back at Oklahoma A&M, following a stint with the Green Bay Packers, joined the Canadian Hamilton Tiger Cats in 1953?

A. Bill Grimes.

Q. Who became the University of Central Oklahoma's head women's volleyball coach in 1990, and was named Lone Star Conference Coach of the Year for 1994?

A. Mark Herrin.

Q. What University of Tulsa female athlete set a school record of 43'3" in shot put in 1993 and one of 123'5" for discus in 1994?

A. Jennifer Swanson.

Q. What bull-riding champion, upon whose life the movie *8 Seconds* was based, is buried at Mt. Olive Cemetery in Hugo?

A. Lane Frost.

Q. In 1981, what Oklahoma catcher was drafted by the Oakland Athletics from the College World Series?

A. Mickey Tettleton.

Q. What 1950s basketball guard at Oklahoma State University returned to the school as head basketball coach in 1990?

A. Eddie Sutton.

Q. Featuring memorabilia from the life of one of the New York Giants' all-time great pitchers, where is the Carl Hubbell Museum?

A. Meeker.

Q. What town is host to the Grady County Rodeo in mid-June and the Grady County Fair the last week of August?

A. Chickasha.

Q. Where did linebacker Matt Monger play college football before joining the New York Jets in 1985, and later the Buffalo Bills?

A. Oklahoma State University.

Q. What Tulsa native set an all-time state amateur record by winning seven state golf championships?

A. Dale McNamara.

Q. What Oklahoma City resident was the national amateur tennis champion for 1940?

A. Don McNeill.

Q. What annual Anadarko event is the nation's oldest Indian-owned and operated fair?

A. American Indian Exposition.

Q. In mid-September, where is the PRCA-sanctioned Great Plains Rodeo held?

A. Altus.

Q. What two-time All-American University of Oklahoma wide receiver was named Most Valuable Player in the 1972 Sugar Bowl?

A. Tinker Owens.

Q. Where was baseball slugger Dale Mitchell born?

A. Colony.

Q. What Panhandle town is host to the World Cow Chip Throwing Championship?

A. Beaver.

Q. What Oklahoma State University baseball All-American played with the Baltimore Orioles in 1984, 1986, and 1988?

A. Jim Traber.

Q. What world champion boxer once ran a rooming house in Sayre?

A. Jess Willard.

Q. Which university's sports teams are nicknamed the Golden Eagles?

A. Oral Roberts University, Tulsa.

Q. What Oklahoman was the PRCA World Champion Steerwrestler for 1985, 1990, 1991, and 1995?

A. Ote Berry.

Q. Running back Elvis Peacock joined what NFL team in 1978, following his college career at the University of Oklahoma?

A. Los Angeles Rams.

Q. What two major gaming centers are operated by Native Americans in the Tulsa area?

A. Cherokee Nation Bingo Outpost and Creek Nation Tulsa Bingo.

Q. The quirky old Route 66 attraction, "The Blue Tourist Whale," can be seen in what town?

A. Catoosa.

SCIENCE & NATURE

CHAPTER SIX

Q. What Oklahoma oil baron's petroleum company once accounted for 10% the world's production of oil?

A. Ernest Whitworth Marland.

———∞———

Q. At 4,973 feet above sea level, what is the highest promontory in the state?

A. Black Mesa (northwest Cimarron County).

———∞———

Q. Where is the largest collection of rhododendrons in the midwest?

A. Lendonwood Gardens (Grove).

———∞———

Q. What Weatherford-born astronaut participated in the Gemini VI, Gemini IX, Apollo X, and Apollo-Soyoz space missions?

A. General Thomas P. Stafford.

———∞———

Q. What 146-acre state park is situated on the north shores of Lake Tenkiller?

A. Cherokee Landing State Park.

Q. Every night during warm months, the bats that inhabit Selman Bat Cave consume how many tons of mosquitoes and other insects?

A. Ten.

———✸———

Q. What marsupial is native to the state?

A. Opossum.

———✸———

Q. What attraction at Anadarko was planned by and constructed under the supervision of the University of Oklahoma's Department of Anthropology?

A. Indian City USA.

———✸———

Q. Who established Okmulgee's first glass plant?

A. Dr. L. S. Skelton.

———✸———

Q. What is Oklahoma's official wildflower?

A. Indian blanket.

———✸———

Q. The pink granite pedestals upon which busts of the governors of Oklahoma are displayed in the state capitol's rotunda were mined near what town?

A. Troy.

———✸———

Q. What was the name of Will Rogers' favorite quarterhorse?

A. Comanche.

Q. At what Norman event is the extract of *Theobroma cacao* celebrated?

A. Chocolate Festival.

———∞———

Q. As the forerunner of the Oklahoma Department of Wildlife, the legislature established what agency in 1909 that closed in 1913 only to reopen in 1925?

A. Game and Fish Department.

———∞———

Q. What three types of bats are on Oklahoma's endangered species list?

A. Gray, Indiana, and Ozark Big-Eared.

———∞———

Q. In the early 1940s, what rich Okmulgee oilman, hog rancher, and U.S. Senator from 1924 to 1930 sported some 8,000 head of purebred Hampshire hogs?

A. W. B. Pine.

———∞———

Q. What is the official state animal?

A. American Buffalo (or Bison).

———∞———

Q. The dunes of Little Sahara State Park are comprised mostly of what mineral?

A. Quartz.

Q. What type of fish, weighing a state record 112 pounds, was taken in the tailwaters of Grand Lake in July 1992?

A. Paddlefish.

———∞∞∞———

Q. What is the name of Ponca City's botanical garden?

A. Cann Memorial Garden Center.

———∞∞∞———

Q. Panama in LeFlore County is home to what large power-generating facility that converts Oklahoma coal into steam and electricity?

A. AES Shadey Point.

———∞∞∞———

Q. What is the home of the world's largest stocker and feeder cattle market?

A. Stockyards City (Oklahoma City National Stockyards).

———∞∞∞———

Q. In 1965, what river was designated as the state's first year-round trout stream?

A. Lower Illinois.

———∞∞∞———

Q. What two types of buzzards are found in Oklahoma?

A. Black and turkey.

———∞∞∞———

Q. Situated near Tulsa, what was the first sizable oil deposit discovered and developed in the state?

A. Glenn Pool Field.

Q. What Heavener resident donated land to the state in 1967 for the creation of Runestone State Park?

A. Herbert Z. Ward.

Q. The Foss Reservoir is on what river?

A. Washita.

Q. Situated west of Orienta, the Glass (or Gloss) Mountains receive their name from what mineral that glistens in the sunlight?

A. Selenite (a form of gypsum).

Q. In 1929, what oil company acquired the Marland Refining Company in Ponca City?

A. Continental Oil Company (Conoco).

Q. Scientifically classified as a member of the pea family, Leguminosae, what is Oklahoma's state tree?

A. Redbud (*Cercis canadensis*).

Q. Where may one see a monument to Oklahoma's peanut industry, featuring the "world's largest peanut"?

A. Durant.

Q. What Oklahoma City facility is not just "strictly for the birds," but also for public devotees of pigeons and doves?

A. World of Wings Pigeon Center.

Q. In the south-central part of the state, what mountain group covers an area approximately 20 by 60 miles?

A. Arbuckle Mountains.

Q. What town is known as the "Trout Capital of Oklahoma"?

A. Gore.

Q. Due to the opening of the East Texas oil fields, to what all-time-low price did Oklahoma oil drop in 1931?

A. A dime per barrel.

Q. What three types of poisonous snakes are found in the state?

A. Copperhead, rattlesnake, and cottonmouth.

Q. Since the State Game and Fish Commission has kept records, what is the weight of the largest alligator gar to be caught in Oklahoma?

A. 153 pounds (Red River, 1991).

Q. What three major tributaries connect to the Arkansas River as it flows through Oklahoma?

A. Canadian, Cimarron, and Neosho (or Grand) Rivers.

Q. What nickname was given the 1941 oil well drilled in a flowerbed directly south of the state capitol?

A. "Petunia #1."

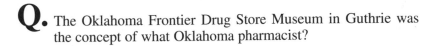

Q. The Oklahoma Frontier Drug Store Museum in Guthrie was the concept of what Oklahoma pharmacist?

A. Ralph Enix.

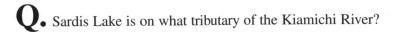

Q. Sardis Lake is on what tributary of the Kiamichi River?

A. Jackfork Creek.

Q. At Vinita in 1905 and again at Watts in 1930, what record low temperature was set for Oklahoma?

A. Minus 27 degrees Fahrenheit (minus 33 degrees Celsius).

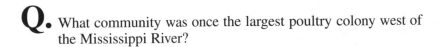

Q. What community was once the largest poultry colony west of the Mississippi River?

A. Nicoma Park.

Q. What facility at Enid functions as one of four flight training centers for the United States Air Force?

A. Vance Air Force Base.

Q. An oil field near Ames consisting of 65 wells is drilled in what eight-mile-wide geological feature, estimated at 600 million years old?

A. An ancient meteor crater.

Q. What town has an iris festival in May?

A. Ponca City.

Q. The U.S. Fish and Wildlife Service first stocked what game fish in Oklahoma Territory in 1895?

A. Rainbow trout.

Q. Lake Eucha, just south of Jay, is owned and operated as the main source of water for which municipality?

A. City of Tulsa.

Q. What dairy product is honored in an annual fall festival in Watonga?

A. Cheese.

Q. The Oklahoma Botanical Gardens and Arboretum complex is on what university campus?

A. Oklahoma State University, Stillwater.

Q. In use since the heyday of the oil boom, where is the world's first spherical oil field storage tank?

A. Davenport.

Q. What is Oklahoma's official state fish?

A. White bass (or sand bass).

Q. The Oklahoma Department of Wildlife has designated what large reptile as threatened in the state?

A. American alligator.

Q. A syrup made from boiling the sap from a member of the grass family is the subject of what annual event at Wewoka?

A. Sorghum Day.

Q. How many exotic animals are on display at the Oklahoma City Zoo?

A. Nearly 22,600.

Q. What Oklahoma town is known as the "Pipeline Crossroads of the World"?

A. Cushing.

Q. What 1,713-acre state park is on the 14,220-acre Broken Bow Lake?

A. Hochatown State Park.

Q. Where is the Kirkpatrick Science and Air Space Museum?

A. Omniplex, Oklahoma City.

━━━◇◇◇━━━

Q. Where in Oklahoma may one of three remaining balloon hangers in the nation be seen?

A. Fort Sill.

━━━◇◇◇━━━

Q. What is the largest oil and gas field in the state?

A. Oklahoma City Field.

━━━◇◇◇━━━

Q. In the 1930s, the Civilian Conservation Corp built what state park on the North Canadian River near Woodward?

A. Boiling Springs State Park.

━━━◇◇◇━━━

Q. What facility completed in Norman in 1999 displays a permanent collection of dinosaur fossils, Oklahoma plant and animal life, along with Native-American art, and Greek and Roman antiquities?

A. Sam Noble Oklahoma Museum of Natural History.

━━━◇◇◇━━━

Q. Consisting of 12 earthen mounds in LeFlore County, what Native-American archaeological site has been called the "King Tut of the West"?

A. Spiro Mounds Archaeological Park.

Q. An 1834 Choctaw tribal law forbade the cutting of what two types of trees?

A. Pecan and hickory.

Q. From what lake was a 44-pound, 12-ounce, state-record grass carp taken in 1994?

A. Arbuckle.

Q. Where is the only place in the world that rockhounds can dig for selenite hourglass crystals?

A. Salt Plains in Alfalfa County.

Q. In 1950, what type of fish was stocked in Canton Reservoir and Tenkiller Reservoir?

A. Walleye.

Q. The Woolaroc Museum and Wildlife Preserve is situated on what oil baron's former ranch?

A. Frank Phillips.

Q. Where was astronaut Gordon Cooper born?

A. Shawnee.

Q. In 1966, the Oklahoma Wildlife Department started work on establishing what large fowl in the state?

A. Canada geese.

Q. What type of fish was introduced into the state at Lake Thunderbird in 1985?

A. Saugeye.

Q. In hopes of re-establishing a permanent presence in the state, what type of deer has been reintroduced in the Glass Hills area?

A. Mule deer.

Q. With over 600 miles of shoreline and 102,000 surface acres, what is the largest man-made lake in the state?

A. Eufaula.

Q. What is the only game fish in the state that may be used for bait?

A. Trout.

Q. Between 1935 and 1940, how many miles of ten-row belts of trees were planted as windbreaks in an attempt to control soil erosion?

A. Some 2,500.

Q. What is the official state rock?

A. Sand barite rosette (rose rock).

Q. The Wichita Mountains are a part of what mountain range?

A. Amarillo.

Q. In 1925, what type of animals came under state regulation and protection for the first time in the state's history?

A. Furbearing mammals.

———∞———

Q. Where is the Aerospace America International Air Show held?

A. Will Rogers World Airport, Oklahoma City.

———∞———

Q. The wood of what native tree, known for its large, bumpy green fruit, was prized by Indians for bow-making?

A. Osage orange (or bois d'arc).

———∞———

Q. What lake serves as a water supply for Norman, Midwest City, and Del City?

A. Thunderbird.

———∞———

Q. Who is believed to have inscribed the 10-by-12-foot runestone near Heavener some one thousand years ago?

A. Scandinavian explorers.

———∞———

Q. What Oklahoman was the first astronaut to be sent twice into orbit?

A. Gordon Cooper.

Q. The fruit of what vine-producing plant, which was widely cultivated by Native Americans, is the subject of a fall celebration in Cordell?

A. Pumpkin.

Q. What stream feeds the waters of the famous Turner Falls?

A. Honey Creek.

Q. Where may the world's largest working cash register be seen?

A. Enterprise Square, USA (Oklahoma City).

Q. In the 1920s, who was the owner of the largest one-man oil company in the world?

A. Lew Wentz.

Q. What lake did the Soil Conservation Service complete near Okmulgee in 1980?

A. Dripping Springs.

Q. Where are almost 50 percent of the 3M Company's computer diskettes manufactured?

A. Weatherford.

Q. What state game farm is located just northwest of El Reno?

A. Darlington Game Bird Hatchery.

Q. Excluding the pink and black granite of its base, the outside of the state capitol is constructed of what material?

A. Indiana limestone.

Q. In Cherokee cuisine, what is the name of a hominy made of corn and nuts?

A. Conutchcie.

Q. What name was given to the region, including Oklahoma, which was stricken by sustained drought and extensive soil erosion in the early 1930s?

A. Dust Bowl.

Q. Altus Reservoir is on what river?

A. North Fork of the Red River.

Q. What two counties contain portions of the Quachita National Forest?

A. LeFlore and McCurtain.

Q. In 1930, what Medford-born Navy flier set an altitude record of 43,165 feet?

A. Apollo Soucek.

Q. What two species of squirrel are found in Oklahoma?

A. Eastern red and eastern gray.

Q. Near the western border with Texas, the South Canadian River does a sharp bend around what irregular gypsum peaks?

A. Antelope Hills.

Q. When was the last wild buffalo herd reported in Oklahoma?

A. 1876.

Q. Located in southern Choctaw County, what is the largest natural lake in the state?

A. Roebuck.

Q. What reptilian roundup is held each April at Mangum?

A. Rattlesnake Derby.

Q. A state-record five-pound, seven-ounce American eel was landed from what river in 1995?

A. Lower Illinois.

Q. What city's annual Azalea Festival features over 30,000 azalea plants in some 625 varieties?

A. Muskogee.

Q. What state park located south of Waynoka near the Cimarron River features sand dunes 25 to 75 feet in height?

A. Little Sahara.

Q. At Frederick, what mollusk is the center of attention on the third Saturday in February?

A. Oyster (for the Annual Oyster Fry).

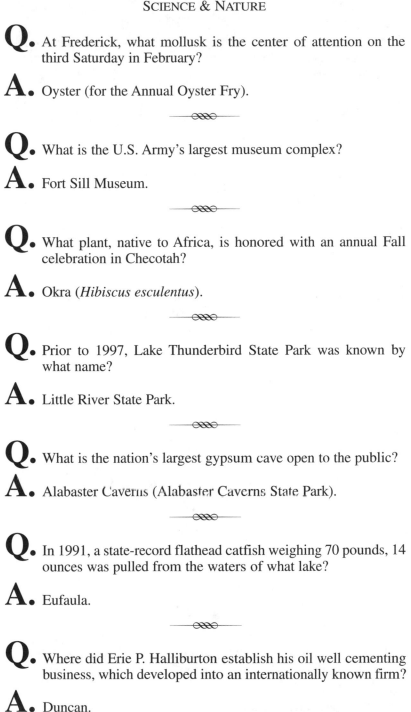

Q. What is the U.S. Army's largest museum complex?

A. Fort Sill Museum.

Q. What plant, native to Africa, is honored with an annual Fall celebration in Checotah?

A. Okra (*Hibiscus esculentus*).

Q. Prior to 1997, Lake Thunderbird State Park was known by what name?

A. Little River State Park.

Q. What is the nation's largest gypsum cave open to the public?

A. Alabaster Caverns (Alabaster Caverns State Park).

Q. In 1991, a state-record flathead catfish weighing 70 pounds, 14 ounces was pulled from the waters of what lake?

A. Eufaula.

Q. Where did Erie P. Halliburton establish his oil well cementing business, which developed into an internationally known firm?

A. Duncan.

Q. What variety of sugar maple, which normally occurs in the Ozark and Quachita Mountains, is found in Red Rock Canyon State Park?

A. Caddo Maple.

Q. Impounding some 8,800 surface acres of water, what is the largest lake in western Oklahoma?

A. Foss Reservoir.

Q. What is the primary type of bat that comprises the two million-plus population of the Selman Bat Cave at Alabaster Caverns State Park?

A. Mexican free-tailed.

Q. In the summer of 1936, what record high temperature for Oklahoma was set at Alva, Altus, and Poteau?

A. 120 degrees Fahrenheit (49 degrees Celsius).

Q. What is the average depth of the Great Salt Plains Lake?

A. Approximately four feet.

Q. When completed in 1941, what was the longest multiple-arch dam in the world?

A. The Grand River Dam.

Q. What 32,000-acre government wildlife area is in Alfalfa County?

A. Salt Plains Federal Wildlife Refuge.

———∞———

Q. What plant festival is held each June in Ponca City?

A. Herb Festival.

———∞———

Q. Located in both Roger Mills and Beckham Counties, what is the name of the world's first upstream flood prevention project?

A. Sand Creek.

———∞———

Q. What prize-winning variety of corn was developed in Seminole County in 1926?

A. Oklahoma Silvermine.

———∞———

Q. What state park, just south of Bragg, is known as "Oklahoma's Sleeping Beauty"?

A. Greenleaf.

———∞———

Q. Measuring 134 feet in height and 3 miles in length, what is the world's largest earthen dam?

A. Foss Reservoir Dam.

———∞———

Q. Approximately how many migratory ducks, geese, and other waterfowl make Sequoyah National Wildlife Refuge near Vian their winter home?

A. Nearly two million.

Q. What is the nickname of the giant 280mm artillery piece that dominates Fort Sill Museum's Cannon Walk?

A. "Atomic Annie."

———∞∞———

Q. A one-acre brine pool at the Cargill Salt Plant near Freedom annually produces how many tons of salt through evaporation?

A. Approximately 1,000.

———∞∞———

Q. What was the first man-made lake to be created in northeastern Oklahoma?

A. Spavinaw.

———∞∞———

Q. What river yielded a record 30-pound channel catfish in 1974 and a record 84-pound blue catfish in 1990?

A. Washita.

———∞∞———

Q. What promontory at Poteau is billed as the "world's highest hill"?

A. Cavanal Hill.

———∞∞———

Q. From 1941 to 1944, the U.S. Army used what Alfalfa County geological oddity for a bombing and strafing range?

A. The Great Salt Plains.

———∞∞———

Q. What geological feature is the repository of the world's largest known deposit of natural gas?

A. Anadarko Basin.

Q. What lake on the North Canadian River was created in 1916 to provide water for Oklahoma City?

A. Overholser (named for Mayor Ed Overholser).

Q. What early 1930s governor shut down production at 3,106 oil wells for three months in an attempt to stabilize plummeting oil prices?

A. William H. Murray.

Q. To service the railroad's needs during the heyday of train travel, where was Oklahoma's largest ice plant constructed?

A. Waynoka.

Q. What three types of rabbit are found in Oklahoma?

A. Cottontail, swamp, and blacktailed jackrabbit.

Q. What is the average annual rainfall in the Panhandle?

A. 15 inches.

Q. The Dalton Caves, where, according to legend, the Dalton gang hid some of their bank and train robbery loot, are along what stream near Sand Springs?

A. Shell Creek.

Q. What beetle is listed as an endangered species in Oklahoma?

A. American burying beetle.

Q. In 1901, what natural disaster forced hundreds of farmers around the community of Blackburn to abandon their homesteads?

A. Drought.

Q. What colorful waterfowl, found in the eastern part of the state, nests in tree cavities and makes an unusual squealing sound?

A. Wood duck.

Q. During the 1930s and 1940s, what Payne County resident developed a small herd of midget milch cows?

A. Otto Gray.

Q. What parasitic plant is Oklahoma's official state flower?

A. Mistletoe (*Phoradendron flavescens*).

Q. Although rarely seen in the early 1900s, through proper wildlife management, what was the estimated population of whitetail deer in Oklahoma in the 1990s?

A. About 400,000.

Q. What heavy metals were first mined in Ottawa County in 1890?

A. Lead and zinc.

Q. Threading its way through the Winding Stair Mountains, what is the only road in the state built expressly for its scenic view?

A. Talimena National Scenic Byway.

Q. What museum in Noble is dedicated to the state rock?

A. Timberlake Rose Rock Museum.

Q. From what lake was a record 38-pound freshwater drum taken in 1976?

A. Tenkiller.

Q. What Bryan County town is host to an annual Magnolia Festival?

A. Durant.

Q. The tornadoes that struck Woodward in April 1947 injured over 1,000 people and took how many lives?

A. 101.

Q. What tree-dwelling amphibian found across much of Oklahoma is known as "the chameleon of the frog world"?

A. Gray tree frog.

Q. In 1886, who became the first person to secure an oil lease with the Cherokee Nation?

A. Edward Byrd.

Q. What town advertises itself as the "Huckleberry Capital of the World"?

A. Jay.

———∞———

Q. The salt produced by natural evaporation at the Cargill Salt Company near Freedom has what high degree of purity?

A. At least 99.6 percent.

———∞———

Q. What 16,000-acre wildlife area is situated near Woodward?

A. Hal and Fern Cooper Wildlife Management Area.

———∞———

Q. Who began mining coal in the Choctaw Nation in 1872?

A. J. J. McAlester.

———∞———

Q. What lizard is the official state reptile?

A. Mountain boomer.

———∞———

Q. For whom is Mount Scott in the Wichita Mountains named?

A. General Winfield Scott.

———∞———

Q. What ground-burrowing member of the squirrel family, noted for living in "towns," is native to Oklahoma?

A. Prairie dog.

Q. The area around Vici is known for what clay material that has been used in cosmetics and in the refining of crude oil?

A. Bentonite.

Q. With as many as ten million birds descending on the area each October, where is the world's largest crow roost?

A. Fort Cobb Recreation Area.

Q. Due to loopholes in Choctaw and federal laws pertaining to prohibition, Krebs became known for what brew manufactured from hops, barley, firsh berries, tobacco, and alcohol?

A. Choctaw or "choc" beer.

Q. What diminutive raptor, found throughout the state, is sometimes call "blue darter"?

A. Cooper's hawk.

Q. At what facility located just southwest of Erick may one visit a bee museum and honey workshop?

A. OK Honey Farm.

Q. For several years following World War I, what Oklahoma county was the banner national wheat producer?

A. Texas County.

Q. What type of material, some 20 to 70 feet thick, caps Black Mesa?

A. Lava.

———— ❈ ————

Q. In 1886, what communication system was installed between Tahlequah and Fort Gibson by Ed Hicks?

A. Telephone line.

———— ❈ ————

Q. In 1919, what became the first commercial venture to reclaim salt by evaporation from brine water pumped from wells on the banks of the Cimarron River northwest of Freedom?

A. Santa Fe Salt Company.

———— ❈ ————

Q. What wildlife facility features such exhibits as Noble Aquatic Center: Aquaticus, Dan Moran Aviary, Butterfly Garden, Herpetarium, Cat Forest/Lion Overlook, and Great Escape?

A. The Zoo, Oklahoma City.

———— ❈ ————

Q. In 1905, the New York Zoological Society donated how many buffalo to the federal government, which, in turn, were relocated to the Wichita Mountains area?

A. 15.

———— ❈ ————

Q. In 1915, the Cushing Oilfield attained a peak gross production of how many barrels of crude oil per day?

A. 305,000.

Q. With the proliferation of farms across the state in the early 1900s, and the cultivation of large areas of land, what burrowing, insect-eating, boney-plated mammal invaded the state from the south?

A. Armadillo.

Q. What 3,522-acre mountainous recreation area includes the Broken Bow Reservoir?

A. Beavers Bend Resort State Park.

Q. What astronaut was born in Okemah?

A. William R. Pogue.

Q. At the peak of its operation, what Oklahoma firm maintained the world's largest zinc smelter?

A. Blackwell Zinc Company.

Q. What attraction, located just south of Davis, bills itself as "Oklahoma's Premier Exotic Animal Theme Park"?

A. Arbuckle Wilderness.

Q. At 77 feet in height, what is the largest waterfall in the state?

A. Turner Falls.

Q. What Carter County oil field produced over 200 million barrels of crude oil between 1913 and 1937?

A. Healdton Oilfield.

Q. Tenkiller Ferry Dam impounds the waters of what river?

A. Illinois.

Q. What is the state bird?

A. Scissor-tailed flycatcher (*Milvulus forficatus*).

Q. In 1927, what breed of cattle was introduced to the Wichita Mountain Wildlife Refuge?

A. Texas longhorns.

Q. During the peak production year of 1920, how many tons of coal were mined in Oklahoma?

A. 4,848,288.

Q. In the decade following statehood, what was Oklahoma's largest cash crop?

A. Cotton.

Q. In 1924, what lake and connecting water system began providing Tulsa with a reliable and sanitary water supply?

A. Spavinaw (Spavinaw Water System).

Q. Shortly after the founding of Okemah in 1902, the town was completely encircled with barbed-wire to protect it from what element on the surrounding prairie?

A. Thousands of longhorn steers.

Q. Whose work in plant breeding during the first part of the twentieth century earned him the title of "Oklahoma Burbank"?

A. Fred Groff.

Q. In 1938, the Oklahoma Game and Fish Commission began restocking what game bird in the state?

A. Quail.

Q. Completed near Chelsea in 1889, what was the depth of the first oil well to be drilled on Cherokee Nation lands?

A. 36 feet.

Q. What name is given to two piles of sandstone boulders placed near Waurika by drovers as a marker on the Chisholm Trail?

A. Monument Rock.

Q. Where does Oklahoma rank in number of horses per capita and in number of horses per square mile in comparison to the other states?

A. First.

Q. The 2,800-acre Sequoyah State Park is situated in what hills west of Wagoner?

A. Cookson Hills.

Q. When the Oklahoma State Board of Pharmacy was formed, who was issued the first certificate as a practicing pharmacist?

A. Foress B. Little.

Q. What commercial ostrich breeding facility at Cartwright also features emu, rhea, and red deer?

A. C B Exotics.

Q. Lake Wister in LeFlore County was created in 1948 as a flood control project on what river?

A. Poteau.

Q. What Cimarron County geological attraction on the Old Santa Fe Trail became a repository of pioneer travelers' graffiti?

A. Autograph Rock.

Q. The Tulsa Port of Catoosa on the Arkansas River McClellan-Kerr Waterway is how many feet in elevation above its conjunction with the Mississippi River?

A. 420 feet.

Q. In 1850, what type of fever outbreak caused the Wichita tribe to move east from the area of present-day Fort Sill to Rush Springs?

A. Malaria.

———⊗⊗⊗———

Q. What 19,364-acre recreation area west of Stillwater is operated by Oklahoma State University?

A. Lake Carl Blackwell.

———⊗⊗⊗———

Q. Though scientifically listed as a member of the rose family, what small fruiting plant is the subject of an annual festival in Stilwell?

A. Strawberry.

———⊗⊗⊗———

Q. What Wewoka African-American attorney founded Black Panther Oil Company, one of the first black-owned petroleum firms in the state?

A. J. Coody Johnson.

———⊗⊗⊗———

Q. Sardis Lake was formerly known by what name?

A. Clayton Lake.

———⊗⊗⊗———

Q. Before the first well drilled in the Oklahoma City Oil Field could be capped, how many barrels of crude oil gushed out of the ground?

A. 110,496.

Q. What insect is a major source of food for the hundreds of thousands of migratory shore birds that pass through the Salt Plains Wildlife Refuge each year?

A. Salt brine flies.

Q. Due to the type of lumber used in its construction, the first bank in Madill was given what name?

A. Cottonwood National.

Q. Over 1,800 horses compete at what event held each November at the State Fairgrounds in Oklahoma City?

A. World Champion Quarter Horse Show.

Q. Where is a replica of the original rig of the first commercial oil well in the state?

A. Johnstone Park, Bartlesville.

Q. What lake is included in the Black Mesa State Park?

A. Carl Etling.

Q. What Oklahoma town was once known as the "Broom Corn Capital of the United States"?

A. Shattuck.